ANIMAL WATCH

A Visual Introduction to

PENGUINS

ANIMAL WATCH

A Visual Introduction to

PENGUINS

A Cherrytree Book

Created by Firecrest Books Ltd
Copyright © 2002 Evans Brothers Ltd
First paperback edition published 2002

First UK edition published 2000
by Cherrytree Press
327 High Street
Slough, Berkshire SL1 1TX

A subsidiary of Evans Brothers Limited

British Library Cataloguing in Publication Data

Stonehouse, Bernard
Penguins. – (Animal watch)
1.Penguins – Juvenile literature
2.Penguins – Behaviour – Juvenile literature
I.Title
599.8

ISBN 1 84234 117 0

Printed and bound in Spain

ANIMAL WATCH

A Visual Introduction to

PENGUINS

Bernard Stonehouse

Illustrated by Martin Camm

CHERRYTREE BOOKS

PICTURE CREDITS

Art and editorial direction by **Peter Sackett**

Edited by **Norman Barrett**

Designed by **Paul Richards, Designers & Partners**

Picture research by **Lis Sackett**

CONTENTS

WHAT IS A PENGUIN

Penguins are birds – warm-blooded and covered with feathers, with bills and clawed feet. They lay eggs and hatch out their young, just like any other bird. Their wings are flippers, too narrow to support them in the air, but strong enough to propel

Emperor penguins

them through the water. Instead of flying, penguins swim fast and dive deep. Some of the bigger ones can dive to over 400 m (1,300 ft) – deeper than any other birds. With the exception of some Galapagos penguins (see page 12), they all live south of the equator, close to the sea where they catch their food. Some spend several months a year at sea, coming ashore only to breed and rear their young.

INTRODUCING THE PENGUINS

Sea-birds that swim and dive, but cannot fly.

PENGUINS ARE a family of sea-birds. There are 18 different species, or kinds, of penguins. They spend part of their life in the sea and part on land, but they cannot fly. At sea, where they are less easy for us to see, they are superbly equipped for swimming and diving. Ashore, they seem clumsy and heavy, shuffling along on short legs. They may waddle as far as the water's edge – but when they dive in, they suddenly turn into sleek, efficient underwater swimmers. The water supports their weight, their clumsiness disappears, and they twist and turn with flippers vibrating, neck stretched and bill snapping.

The macaroni penguin illustrated here, from South Georgia, has found a shoal of shrimp-like krill just below the surface. Darting back and forth, it snaps them up and swallows them as it goes. Every minute or so it will shoot to the surface for a quick breath of air, then dive again to continue feeding.

Penguins have to swim as fast and efficiently as the fish, shrimps and other sea-animals on which they live. Their main enemies also live in the water. Simply to stay alive, penguins must be able to out-swim some of the fastest seals and predatory fish.

Macaroni penguin swimming through a shoal of krill

Below: Penguins are very much at home in the water

RELATIONSHIPS

Penguin flipper (top) and guillemot wing. The flipper is for swimming only; the wing is for flying and swimming.

Penguin   *Guillemot*

The penguins form a family of their own that biologists call the Spheniscidae. We do not know which other birds are their nearest relations. Although penguins cannot fly, it is known, from the bones of their flippers and other clues, that they evolved long ago from flying birds (see pages 11 and 13).

Penguins look very much like guillemots, diving birds of a different family that live in the northern hemisphere. Both can stand upright and both have a streamlined shape and small wings. But similarity does not make them closely related. The birds have come to look like each other simply because they both catch their food by swimming and they both have evolved the most efficient shape for this way of life.

SPECIES DIFFERENCES

Apart from size, the bodies of all penguins – with dark backs and pale fronts – look very much alike. The differences between the species appear mainly on the heads and necks.

In the water, the dark backs and pale bellies make it hard for seals or other predators to see penguins, either from below against the bright sky, or from above against the dark sea. This applies to all penguins, wherever they are.

When several different kinds of penguin are swimming together and looking to join others of their own kind, they have to look at heads and necks above the water surface to see characteristics that distinguish one species from another.

Gentoo

Rockhopper

Penguins at the surface

IS IT A PENGUIN?
You always know a penguin when you see one. They stand upright on short legs, with flippers by their sides. The chest and shirt-front are usually white, the head and back blue-grey or black. The different species have distinguishing markings – bands of dark feathers across their front, yellow or golden patches on the head, crests of bright golden feathers over the eyes.

Most penguins live in groups, some in colonies of thousands. A lone penguin coming out of the sea will call, then walk over to join the nearest group of penguins.

If there are people about, it is just as likely to walk up and stand among them. It needs the company, and sees humans as just another kind of penguin.

Penguins on land

Explorers and travellers who first met penguins saw them as clumsy and inefficient on land. Hungry sailors killed many for fresh meat, thinking them stupid because they were not afraid and could not fly away. However, despite their short legs and fat bodies, penguins get by very well ashore. Many walk several kilometres inland over snow or rough ground to reach their nests. The smaller species hop, scramble and climb up steep cliffs, using their beaks, flippers and claws. Polar penguins grip the ice with their claws and 'toboggan' on their stomachs over soft snow (see page 23). The burrowing penguins dig tunnels for themselves like rabbits (see page 35).

Penguins have few enemies on land and are often unafraid of people, so they stay by their nests when visitors approach. Yet a frightened penguin can run much faster than a human over snow and rocky ground.

Penguins entering the water from an iceberg

BREEDING
Like all other birds, penguins lay eggs and incubate them. Their eggs are white, often with a chalky outer shell and blue lining. Emperor and king penguins, the two largest species, build no nests. They lay only a single egg, which they hold on their feet. All other kinds build nests on the ground, usually of stones, moss, grass or old bones, and lay two eggs. In most species the two eggs are of similar size. The six species of crested penguins lay two eggs of

different sizes, the first noticeably smaller than the second. In all species but one, both parents share incubation. Among emperors, only the male incubates the egg.

Penguin chicks look nothing like their parents. They are covered with thick woolly down. When the chicks are very small, one parent broods them and keeps them warm, while the other hunts for food. Later, the chicks are left alone, and both parents hunt at the same time. To feed their chicks, penguins bring home food in their crop (the first, sac-like part of their stomach) and feed it by regurgitation – that is, by bringing it up bit by bit into the back of the throat, from where the chick takes it.

Most species of penguins manage to raise their chicks in a summer of four or five months. Emperors take eight or nine months to raise their chicks. Kings take over a year. When the chicks are grown and ready for the sea, they moult into a juvenile plumage of feathers, similar to that of adults but paler. One year later they moult again, this time into full adult plumage.

Adélie penguin colony

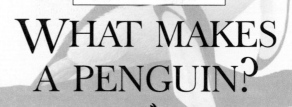

FLYING, SWIMMING AND DIVING

Some flying birds, such as diving ducks and gannets, swim by paddling with their feet, holding their wings close to their sides. They cannot swim fast or dive deep.

Guillemots, puffins and grebes use their wings and powerful wing muscles underwater, letting their feet trail behind to act as rudders. Their wings are big enough for flying if they flap them very fast, and they cannot soar or glide. They swim and dive more efficiently than 'foot-swimmers', but again only just.

Penguins are 'wing-swimmers' whose ancestors, long ago, gave up flying to swim and dive more efficiently. The big muscles that operate their flippers are the same as those that operate the wings of flying birds. The flippers contain the same bones as flying wings, only flattened and strengthened.

Penguin 'flying' under water

WHAT MAKES A PENGUIN?

How penguins are adapted for life at sea and on land.

I LLUSTRATED HERE are the biggest and smallest living penguins, and a giant penguin of the past. Emperor penguins, the biggest living penguins, stand about 110 cm (43 in) tall and weigh up to 41 kg (90 lb). Little blue penguins, the smallest, stand little more than a third as tall, and weigh just over 1 kg (2 lb 3oz).

Why are some penguins big and others small? Big penguins find it easier to keep warm, because they produce more heat in their muscles and can hold their heat in more efficiently. So the bigger penguins live in cool or cold climates, the smaller ones in warmer areas. However, big penguins can also dive deeper and stay down longer than small penguins. The smallest penguins feed almost entirely in surface waters. Bigger ones catch food far below the surface. This may be a more important reason why they come in different sizes.

The largest penguins − like the one represented below − are no longer living. They are known only from fossil bones. Several species were much bigger than today's emperors. One in particular stood more than 1.5 m (5 ft) tall, and probably weighed over 100 kg (220 lb).

Giant penguins of the past were about this size, but we do not know what they looked like

WHAT DO THEY EAT?

Penguins feed only at sea. Some feed mainly on shrimp-like crustaceans or small fish, which they catch near the surface. Others, including most of the bigger ones, dive deeper to feed on larger fish and squid. Their bills are sharp-edged, mostly with a hook at the end. The tongue and lining of the mouth have backward-pointing spines. Once caught, prey are very unlikely to wriggle free and escape.

Like all other sea-birds, penguins have a wide throat and a sac-like crop or stomach, which they fill with food. The macaroni penguin, for example, which weighs about 4 kg (10 lb), can catch and hold at least 450 g (1 lb) of fish or shrimps in its crop. Usually it digests the food quickly, but if it has a nest ashore, it can carry this amount of food home to feed its chick.

Gentoo penguin feeding its chick by regurgitation

Human explorer 1.8 m (6 ft) tall

PENGUIN EVOLUTION

Guillemots (page 8) show how penguins may have evolved from flying birds. The ancestors of penguins were probably small sea-birds that, like guillemots, could fly, swim and dive. Their wings, with flight feathers along the trailing edge, were big enough to support them in the air, and powerful enough to push them through the water as well. Being able to dive even a few centimetres below the surface allowed them to fish beyond the reach of birds that could not dive at all.

However, flight feathers reduced their speed and efficiency underwater. Some that were born with much smaller flight feathers found that, although they could no longer fly, they were better at swimming and diving. These were the first true penguins.

Once they had given up flight, penguins could become bigger, which helped them to dive deeper. By losing the ability to fly they became the world's most efficient swimming and diving birds.

MALE AND FEMALE PENGUINS

In almost every species of penguins the sexes are very similar. It is hard to tell them apart just by looking at them. Males in each species are usually slightly larger than females, with slightly heavier bills. In any pair at a nest, the one that is slightly taller, with the longer and heavier bill, is almost certainly the male. This difference is most marked in the crested penguins, but often shows up in other species as well.

Another way of telling males from females is by their behaviour. Males usually arrive on the colonies and take up nest sites first. In courtship they are more active and aggressive, more likely to fend off rivals, to make calls that attract partners, and to be involved in fights.

It is possible, too, to tell the sexes by examining the cloaca (vent under the tail), but this involves handling the birds, which makes them frightened and cross, and alters their behaviour. Scientists can also tell by taking a feather and sampling the DNA. Male and female feathers show different patterns. However, this requires a well-equipped laboratory, so is not practical.

Emperor and little blue – the largest and smallest living penguins

Moulting

Feathers are made of material similar to hair and nails, and soft enough to wear out. They have to be replaced at least once a year. While most flying birds moult their feathers in small patches, penguins change theirs all at once, usually after they have finished breeding.

They go to sea for a few days beforehand to fatten up, then come ashore and find a sheltered corner to stand in. Within two or three days they start to look puffy. The new feathers are starting to grow, and pushing the old ones out. Then the old feathers start falling away, showing the tips of the new ones underneath. On a big colony there are feathers everywhere, as though thousands of penguins have been pillow-fighting.

It takes three to four weeks for all the old plumage to be replaced. Then the penguins return to the sea, smart in their clean new suits of feathers, and much slimmer after their long fast.

Moulting penguin

HOW FAST DO THEY SWIM?

Because they are small and lively in the water, penguins seem to dart about very quickly. If you measure their speed alongside a ship or boat, you find that most can swim at up to about 7-8 km/h (4-5 mph), as fast as a good walking pace. They can sprint faster in short bursts. Kings and emperors almost double this speed over short distances. However, when travelling far, for example to and from the feeding grounds, penguins of all sizes swim more slowly, averaging 3.5-7 km/h (2-4 mph).

On long journeys, penguins usually swim together in groups, leaping out of the water every few seconds and diving back in immediately. Because dolphins and porpoises also swim like this, it is called 'porpoising'. Each leap allows them to snatch a breath, taking in the oxygen needed to stay alive, and getting rid of carbon dioxide which would otherwise poison them. In porpoising, penguins swim continuously, a more efficient way than stopping every few seconds to breathe. On long journeys they take resting breaks too, floating or swimming on the surface like ducks.

Penguin porpoising

COLD-SEA AND WARM-SEA PENGUINS

The six genera (see page 14) and 18 species of living penguins fall into two groups, according to the temperature of the seas in which they live.

COLD-SEA PENGUINS
(pages 14–15)

Genus *Aptenodytes*:

Emperor penguin
King penguin

Genus *Pygoscelis*:

Adélie penguin
Chinstrap penguin
Gentoo penguin

Genus *Eudyptes*:

Rockhopper penguin
Macaroni penguin
Royal penguin

Emperor and Adélie penguins live in the coldest regions of the Antarctic coast, with chinstraps and southern populations of gentoos in some of the milder parts. Some stocks of macaronis penetrate to the edges of Antarctica, but most, such as kings, northern gentoos, royals and rockhoppers, feed and breed in the cold temperate zone.

WARM-SEA PENGUINS
(pages 16–17]

Genus *Spheniscus*:

Jackass penguin
Magellanic penguin
Peruvian penguin
Galapagos penguin

Genus *Megadyptes*:

Yellow-eyed penguin

Genus *Eudyptula*:

Little blue penguin
White-flippered penguin

Genus *Eudyptes*:

Erect-crested penguin
Fiordland penguin
Snares penguin

Jackass penguins live off southern Africa, Magellanic penguins off the Falkland Islands and southern South America, Peruvian penguins along the coast of Peru, and Galapagos penguins among the equatorial Galapagos Islands. Little blue penguins live along eastern, southern and western coasts of Australia, and around New Zealand and the nearby Chatham Islands. The remaining five species all live in the waters off southern New Zealand, or islands immediately to the south and east.

WHERE PENGUINS LIVE AND BREED

Nearly all penguins live in the southern hemisphere, always close to the sea.

PENGUINS LIVE almost entirely in the southern hemisphere. Just a few individuals, nesting on the northernmost island of the Galapagos group, have crossed the equator to live a few kilometres within the northern hemisphere. Penguins have two great needs – land on which they can form their nesting colonies and breed, and seas in which they can swim and feed. They live only along coasts, never more than a few kilometres inland, and can breed only in areas that are close to a plentiful food supply. Because they cannot fly, they nest on the ground, and must be free of such land predators as dogs, wolves, cats and humans.

There are no penguins in the Arctic or temperate regions of the northern hemisphere and, so far as we know, there never have been. Penguins evolved in middle latitudes of the southern hemisphere, and only a few species have managed to move north towards the equator. Even these live in the coolest waters they can find. They have not been able to cross the wide belt of warm equatorial waters to get to the cooler oceans in the north. Warm seas contain predatory sharks and other fish big enough to snap up any penguins that come along and cannot escape by flight.

Penguins, including kings and gentoos, have several times been caught in the southern hemisphere and released in the north, mainly around northern Norway, in the hope that they would settle and live there. These experiments have always failed. The birds disappeared after a few weeks. Some may have tried to migrate south. Others may have been taken by land predators, such as bears and foxes, that live in the Arctic but not in the far south.

FOSSIL PENGUINS

Fragments of fossil penguins have been found in South America, South Africa, Australia, New Zealand and Antarctica – all places in the southern hemisphere where penguins live today. No complete skeletons have been found, just individual bones from the feet or flippers, or pieces of skull or breastbone. These fossils show that most of the early penguins were within the size range of modern penguins, though a few were much bigger (see page 10).

So far no fossils have been found representing the smallest or very earliest penguins. Their bones would have been smaller and more fragile than those of the big ones, and less likely to survive as fossils after 35–40 million years. The immediate ancestors of the earliest penguins were probably smaller and lighter than today's little blues, and at that size, still able to fly.

GREAT AUK

A species of large, flightless bird called the great auk, or garefowl, lived in the Arctic for many thousands of years. Related to guillemots and puffins, great auks were diving birds with reduced wings. Like penguins, they had become too heavy to fly. They lived in colonies on islands in the North Atlantic Ocean, where for hundreds of years they were killed by fishermen for food and bait, and robbed of their eggs. By the early 1800s there were very few left, and the last great auks were killed in 1844.

If penguins had lived in the Arctic, they would probably have suffered a similar fate. There would certainly have been fewer of them than there are today.

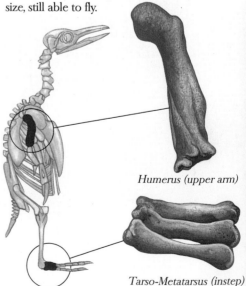

Humerus (upper arm)

Tarso-Metatarsus (instep)

The penguin world

PENGUINS AND THE DRIFTING CONTINENTS

About 150 million years ago, the continents of the world were joined in one big landmass (see below). By 100 million years ago, they had started to drift apart. About 35-40 million years ago, when the first penguins appeared, South America and South Africa were still closer than at present, and Antarctica, Australia and New Zealand had only just begun to separate from each other. The world as a whole was much warmer than it is now. There was no southern ice-cap and no sea ice.

The earliest penguins were swimming in seas at least as warm as those off Australia and northern New Zealand today.

As the continents moved apart, Antarctica drifted south into its present polar position. The southernmost lands and seas all grew colder, and Antarctica became covered with ice. Some kinds of penguins continued to live in the warmer waters, as most do at present. Others found a better living in the colder seas to the south, growing thicker feathers and storing more fat under their skin to help them keep warm.

150 million years ago

100 million years ago

40 million years ago

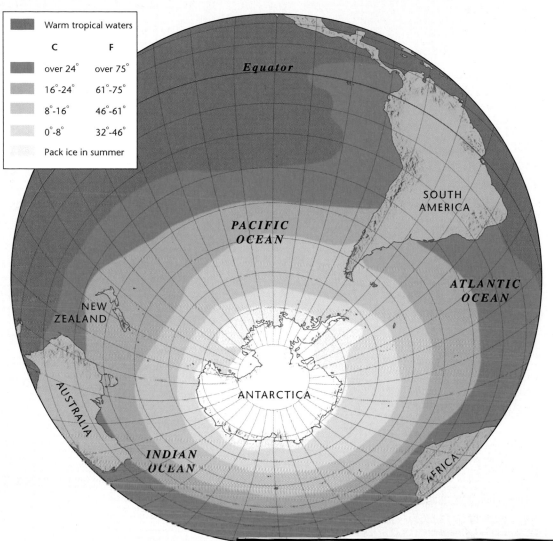

	Warm tropical waters	
	C	**F**
	over 24°	over 75°
	16°-24°	61°-75°
	8°-16°	46°-61°
	0°-8°	32°-46°
	Pack ice in summer	

The map shows the area of the world where penguins live and breed, divided into temperature zones. In their warmest breeding areas – southern Africa, Australia and South America – they feed where the coasts are washed by cool currents, which provide more food than warmer waters. In the cooler regions, they breed mainly on islands, some just offshore, but most in mid-ocean, where they are surrounded by rich feeding areas, especially in summer. Some small islands are almost completely covered with thousands of nests of penguins, albatrosses and other sea-birds. See the maps on pages 19 to 41 for where the individual species live.

Most species of penguins live in middle latitudes. New Zealand and its neighbouring islands in the southern Pacific Ocean and the Falkland Islands in the southern Atlantic Ocean each support five species. Other species prefer warmer or colder waters, including the coldest waters of all, around Antarctica. The highest numbers of penguins, in breeding colonies of tens or hundreds of thousands, are found in the cold waters of the southern oceans.

COLD-SEA PENGUINS

Emperor	King	Adélie	Chinstrap

Gentoo	**Rockhopper**	**Macaroni**	**Royal**

WARM-SEA PENGUINS

Jackass	Magellanic	Peruvian	Galapagos	Yellow-eyed

Little blue	**White-flippered**	**Erect-crested**	**Fiordland**	**Snares**

RELATIONSHIPS

The 18 different kinds of penguins − all the living species − are different enough from all other birds to form an 'order', or major grouping, of their own, the Sphenisciformes. An order usually contains several families, but all penguins past and present are so similar to each other that they are all included in one family, the Spheniscidae.

Penguins turning their backs to the wind

Biologists give each species a scientific name, made up of two words based on Latin or Greek. The first word names the genus (plural, genera), or small group, to which the species belongs, the second is the species' own particular name.

Some species that live over a wide geographical range vary slightly in size, colour or other detail from one area to another. Biologists call these different populations 'subspecies', identifying them by adding a third word to the name (see, for example, gentoo penguins, page 20).

COLD-CLIMATE PENGUINS

Penguins of the polar and sub-polar oceans.

THOUGH MOST PEOPLE think of penguins in a setting of snow and ice, fewer kinds of penguins live in cold seas than in temperate or warm seas. However, some of the polar and sub-polar species are numbered in millions, while most of the temperate and tropical species have much smaller populations.

Penguins choose to live in the coldest seas because cold water is rich in nutrients and food, providing a good living for birds that are well-enough insulated to keep warm.

Of the cold-climate penguins, only emperors, Adélies, chinstraps and southern stocks of gentoo penguins are fully adapted, with thick coats of long feathers and thick blubber, for living in the coldest polar areas. Kings, macaronis, royals and northern gentoos, living only on the fringes of Antarctica, feed in seas that are sometimes as cold as those in the far south, but they never meet the extreme cold of southern lands. So they can manage with less fat and thinner plumage.

King

Adélie

Rockhopper

Chinstrap

Keeping warm in cold climates

KEEPING COOL

If a penguin gets too hot, it increases the blood supply to its skin and the surplus heat escapes into the surroundings. The heat is shed particularly through the flippers and face, which have only

Penguin in a severe snowstorm

tiny feathers and no underlying blanket of fat. In some tropical species, such as Peruvian penguins (pages 38-39), the face is almost bare, allowing them to shed excess heat faster. On land they also open up their feathers to allow heat to escape.

When penguins feel cold, they bask in the sun for warmth, just as we do. When they feel hot, they seek the shade, or return to the sea. While cold-climate penguins always nest in the open, those of warm-temperate and tropical climates nest in burrows, under rocks or in caves to avoid exposure to the hot sun.

Like all other birds, penguins are warm blooded, with a body temperature of about 37°C (99°F). They swim in seas that, even in the tropics, are colder than their bodies, and in polar regions are very much colder. They keep warm, just as we do, by chemical activities in muscles and other tissues.

Their first protection against the cold is their feathers. An adult penguin has 10 or 11 feathers per square centimetre (70 feathers per square inch) on its chest and back – more on its neck, where the feathers are

smaller. Each feather has a patch of down around the base, and grows out from the skin in a curve, so that a layer of air is trapped between the feathers. The trapped air acts as insulation, like the air inside a warm shirt.

The down at the bases of the feathers forms a warm undervest, and the tips of the feathers, overlapping like tiles on a roof, make a watertight and windproof outer covering.

So the skin underneath stays dry and warm, never coming into direct contact with cold sea or rain, and insulated from the cold atmosphere by its layer of air.

Adélie penguins in their natural habitat of ice and snow

1. Feathers open – warm air can escape from expanded blood vessels

2. Feathers closed – warm air trapped and blood supply restricted

Gentoo

Royal

Macaroni

Emperor

KEEPING WARM

Warm climates are not always warm enough, especially for chicks. Penguin chicks just out of the egg have no control over their body temperature. They have to be 'brooded' – held against the parent's body to keep warm – for two to three weeks before they can maintain a constant temperature of their own. This is a very dangerous period for them. If the brooding parent is disturbed and runs away, the chicks are left unguarded and likely to chill.

Even after two or three weeks, when they can maintain their temperature without brooding, chicks are at risk from bad weather. Parental feathers are waterproof and windproof, like a good raincoat. The down that covers chicks is neither. Cold rain and chill winds can penetrate it, cooling the chick faster than it can warm itself up. This happens often in cool climates, and may happen even in the subtropics during long spells of stormy weather.

WARM-CLIMATE PENGUINS

Penguins of temperate and tropical oceans.

PENGUINS of warm climates include all four species of burrowing penguins, which live in South Africa and South America. The other six species live in Australia, New Zealand and neighbouring waters.

These penguins never put on quite so much fat as the cold-climate species. Because their feathers are shorter, they tend to look thinner – less rounded and plump. However, in a line-up of all the penguin species, it would be hard to guess, just by looking at them, which live in cold climates and which in warm.

The reason is that all are adapted for living, sometimes for days or weeks on end, in water that is much colder than they are. Even tropical seas draw heat constantly from their bodies. As a result, all penguins, including those of warm climates, need good, overall insulation. Those that live in colder water need more, and those that brave the coldest lands need more still. But these differences are slight compared with the prime need of every penguin to keep cold water at a distance from its warm skin and underlying muscles.

Yellow-eyed

Jackass

Galapagos

Erect-crested

Snares

White-flippered

Little blue

BLACK AND WHITE

Feather on penguin's back

Most people think of penguins as having black backs and white fronts. That is how they are usually described. However, while most have creamy-white feathers on the breast and abdomen, very few have backs that are truly black.

Almost every feather on the back of every penguin has a blue spot near the tip. In some species the spot is small, giving an overall dark, even black appearance. In others it is much larger, so the back is a blue-grey rather than black. In little blue penguins especially, but also in kings and the juveniles of some macaronis, the blue is stronger than the black, giving the birds a quite pale blue-grey colour.

Penguins look their smartest and best just after moulting (see page 11), when their feathers are new and unworn. They keep their plumage in good order by constant preening, rubbing oil onto their bills from a gland just above the tail, and transferring a tiny smear to each feather in turn. Any penguin ashore with nothing better to do spends time preening its feathers.

However, constant exposure to sun, wind and salt-water frays the tips of the feathers, fading the blue to dull grey and the black to smoky brown. The white shirt-fronts become yellow, and start to look worn. Most adults moult in autumn, as soon as their chicks have reached independence. This gives them a new, unworn suit to start the winter.

Keeping cool in warm climates

To be able to spend many hours, days or weeks at a time at sea, warm-blooded penguins have to be well insulated – hence the very efficient covering, common to all penguins, of feathers and fat (see page 15). However, when the warm-climate penguins are standing or moving about on land, especially under tropical or even temperate-latitude sunshine, keeping warm is not a problem. Their main problem is to keep cool.

Even when sleeping or totally inactive, penguins produce heat within their bodies that keeps them at a comfortable internal temperature. Walking, running, fighting and other muscular activities generate more heat, which they must shed. Some is lost through the surface of the throat and mouth by panting. Some passes out through the skin, especially through the flippers and face, which have the smallest feathers and least insulation (page 15).

Like human divers in wet suits, if they walk, run or stand for long in warm sunshine, they quickly begin to feel overheated. They can pant faster, but that uses water from their bodies, which they may not be able to replace. They can 'turn on their radiators' – that is, increase the flow of blood through the flippers and face. Several of the warm-climate species, notably Peruvian penguins, have faces almost bare of feathers, which turn bright red when they are overheating.

Fiordland penguin

Their main remedy is to avoid strong sunshine. They do this by spending their days at sea and coming ashore only at night. You see them on the beaches mainly in the early morning and late evening. You hear their courtship and mating activities – often very noisy and quarrelsome – during the dark hours. Whereas cold-climate penguins nest in the open, those of warm climates nest in burrows, caves and cavities under rocks or vegetation – any shelter that keeps them out of direct sunshine.

Magellanic

Peruvian

Fiordland

Magellanic penguin at the mouth of its burrow

ADÉLIE PENGUINS

Almost every expedition to the Antarctic continent has met and made friends with these entertaining black and white penguins.

FACT FILE

Order:	Sphenisciformes
Family:	Spheniscidae
Latin name:	*Pygoscelis adeliae*
Colour:	Black head and back, white shirt-front, white ring around eyes
Standing height:	73 cm (29 in)
Flipper length:	17 cm (7 in)
Weight:	Avge* 5 kg (11 lb); up to 8 kg (18 lb)
Breeding range:	Antarctic continental coasts and neighbouring islands

*Average

RELATIONSHIPS

Adélie, gentoo and chinstrap penguins (pages 20-21) are three very closely related species, which together form the genus *Pygoscelis*. The name means 'brush-tailed', referring to the unusually long tail feathers. These sweep the snow behind when it walks upright.

The three species are very similar to each other in both appearance and behaviour. You can tell them apart mainly by the shape and markings of their heads. Adélies have a distinctive white ring around each eye, and feathers growing along the short, almost conical bill. Compare this with the markings of gentoos and chinstraps on the next pages. When alarmed or angry, Adélies raise the feathers on the neck and back of the head to form a crest. Neither of the other species can do this.

All three species form breeding colonies, or rookeries, sometimes of several thousand pairs. Usually they nest separately from each other. In a few places there are colonies of two or even all three species together. Only very rarely have they been known to interbreed. In all species, males are slightly larger than females. You can sometimes see which is which when two are standing together at a nest.

GO ASHORE on almost any island close to Antarctica between late October and March and you are likely to meet Adélie penguins. You seldom see one Adélie on its own. The smallest colonies contain several dozen birds, the largest tens or even hundreds of thousands. Watch by the shore, and you see them coming in from the sea, scuttling up the beach between waves and running to the safety of the upper shore, where they can stand, catch their breath and preen their wet, glistening feathers.

During the nesting season, you see processions of clean, shiny penguins walking inshore towards the colony, and processions of dirtier, scruffier birds making their way back to the sea after incubating or tending their chicks. As each bird reaches the colony, it weaves its way between the nests, dodging the beaks of a hundred neighbours, to find its own nest and partner. Partners always seem pleased to see each other, calling excitedly and displaying. If there are eggs in the nest, the incubating partner will stand up, step aside, and let the newcomer take over. If there are chicks, the newcomer will feed them with fish or shrimps brought from the sea in its crop.

Adélie penguins on ice-floe

The two chicks in each nest, covered with dense, dark-brown down, huddle together for warmth, tended always by one of their parents while the other forages at sea. After three or four weeks, they are big enough to leave the nest, and gather in groups of 20 or more. Then both parents can leave for the sea, bringing back twice as much food.

BREEDING

From late October adults return to the colony where they have nested previously, often the ones in which they were hatched. Males usually return a few days before females, finding the sites where they nested last season. These may still be under snow, in temperatures as low as −20°C (-4°F). They defend their sites against other penguins, which may try to steal them. When the females return, the males attract them to the site by calling. The pair make a small nest of pebbles, bones and moss, and after a few days mate several times. In mating, the female lies in the nest, and the male stands on her back, pressing the underside of his tail to hers, and injecting a package of sperm into her vent. The sperm swim up the oviduct to where two partly formed eggs are

already waiting.
The eggs, now fertilized, pass down the oviduct, acquiring their albumen and shell, and are laid three or four days apart.

Males incubate for the first 10-15 days, while the females return to sea for a feed. Then the females incubate for a few days while the males are feeding, and after that they take turns of two to three days at a time. The eggs hatch after about 34 days, and the parents feed the tiny chicks from part-digested food in their own crops. Fed first by the parents alternately, the silvery-grey chicks grow quickly. After about eight weeks, now almost as big as adults, they grow feathers to replace their down. At nine to ten weeks, they enter the sea for the first time and start to hunt for themselves.

Adélie penguin with chick

FEEDING

Adélie penguins feed mainly on small, shrimp-like crustaceans and young fish, 5-8 cm (2-3 in) long. These form part of the zooplankton, the tiny animals that swarm in surface waters during the summer months. Adélies do not have to swim far or dive deep for their food. They bring home 350 g (12 oz) or more at a time in their crops. But sometimes the food becomes scarce in mid-to-late summer and hundreds of chicks die of starvation.

Adélie penguins braving a blizzard

Where Adélies live

Adélie penguins live mainly along the coasts of Antarctica, wherever they can find islands or stretches of rocky shore. They also breed on many of the islands close to Antarctica that are surrounded by pack-ice in winter, including the South Shetland, South Orkney and South Sandwich islands, Peter I Øy and Scott Island. With Emperor penguins (pages 22-23), they are the coldest-living of all the penguins, often swimming in seas that are part covered with ice-flocs, and breeding among snow and ice on land.

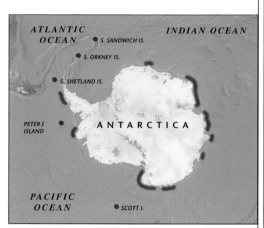

ATLANTIC OCEAN · S. SANDWICH IS. · INDIAN OCEAN
· S. ORKNEY IS.
· S. SHETLAND IS.
PETER I ISLAND · ANTARCTICA
PACIFIC OCEAN · SCOTT I.

▮ Adélie penguins

WHY ADÉLIE?

Adélie penguins were first described by naturalists from a French Antarctic expedition of 1837-40. Led by Capt Dumont d'Urville, the expedition discovered in the far south a small group of islands and a stretch of ice cliff, which the leader thought, quite rightly, must be the coast of a new land. On the islands he found thousands of these little black and white penguins, incubating and feeding their chicks. He called the land 'Terre Adélie' (French for 'Adélie Land') after his wife, and the naturalists gave the same name to the penguins that they found there.

Adélie about to jump into the water

PREDATORS

On land, Adélie penguins battle constantly with skuas – large brown gulls that live close to the colonies and prey constantly upon them. Skuas attack and kill any that are wounded or damaged, and take any unattended eggs or small chicks that they see around the colonies. At sea the main predators are leopard seals, which catch and kill the penguins as they are coming ashore. A leopard seal may catch over a dozen Adélies for a single meal.

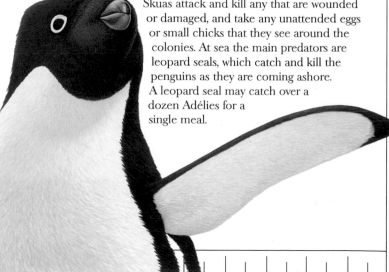

FACT FILE

CHINSTRAP PENGUIN

Family:	Spheniscidae
Latin name:	*Pygoscelis antarctica*
Colour:	Black head and back, white shirt-front, white chin crossed by narrow black band
Standing height:	73 cm (29 in)
Flipper length:	18 cm (7 in)
Weight:	Avge 4.5 kg (10 lb); up to 5.3 kg (12 lb)
Breeding range:	South Orkney, South Shetland and South Sandwich islands, South Georgia, Antarctic Peninsula

GENTOO PENGUIN

Family:	Spheniscidae
Latin name:	*Pygoscelis papua*
Colour:	Black head and back, white shirt-front spotted with black, white patches over eyes and crown, orange-red bill and feet
Standing height:	76 cm (30 in)
Flipper length:	20 cm (8 in)
Weight:	Avge 6 kg (13 lb); up to 7.4 kg (16 lb 5 oz)
Breeding range:	S. Orkney, S. Shetland and S. Sandwich islands, S. Georgia, Antarctic Peninsula, Falklands and many other southern islands

RELATIONSHIPS

Chinstrap penguins are slightly smaller and more slender than Adélie penguins (page 18), with a narrow black line under the eye and chin. Gentoos are taller, with a black face, white bar across the top of the head, and a distinctive orange-red bill and feet.

Chinstraps, like Adélies, are much the same wherever you find them. Gentoos vary: those living in the coldest areas are smaller than those of warmer climates, with shorter bills, flippers and feet. Some biologists call them northern and southern subspecies, naming them *Pygoscelis papua papua* and *Pygoscelis papua ellsworthii*, respectively.

CHINSTRAP AND GENTOO PENGUINS

Fierce and gentle black and white penguins of the far south.

CHINSTRAP AND GENTOO penguins are similar in size to Adélies and at first glance look very much like them. However, there is no mistaking the smart black strap of the chinstrap penguin, or the bright orange bill and feet of the gentoo. Chinstrap chicks are silver-grey all over, gentoo chicks are silvery, but with darker heads.

Their colonies also appear very similar – often hundreds or thousands of nests packed closely together, each with its guardian birds and, later in the season, one or two chicks in each nest. They sound similar, too. Throughout the breeding season there is a constant racket of penguin voices, raised in greeting, invitation or anger. Chinstraps are more raucous than Adélies, and sound like noisy parrots. Gentoos are more musical, like geese. But the noise from any large colony can be deafening.

On warm days there is a strong smell, too, both from the droppings of thousands of birds and from decaying food spilt as the chicks are fed. With the wind in the right direction, you can smell a large colony several kilometres away.

Gentoo and chinstrap penguins usually nest within a few metres of the sea. However, colonies are sometimes found more than a kilometre inland, and 150 m (500 ft) or more above sea level, so the birds have to walk and climb long distances to reach their nests. Gentoos are rather timid and likely to run away when people are around – 'gentle gentoos', they are called. Chinstraps tend to be much more aggressive. They fight more among themselves, and are more likely to attack humans than run away. Penguins attack people like they attack each other – by grasping with the bill and beating hard with both flippers.

Gentoo penguin and chick on a nest

FEEDING

Like Adélie penguins, gentoos and chinstraps feed mainly on zooplankton (see page 19). Gentoos tend to feed closer to shore, and can also dive deeper, to 150 m (500 ft), where they may catch larger fish. Chinstraps can bring home around 600 g (20 oz) of food in their crops, gentoos up to 900 g (2 lb).

BREEDING

Chinstraps and gentoos on the southern islands spend their winters away from the colony areas, probably on the sea ice or farther north. Gentoos on the northern islands are often resident throughout the year. As snow levels fall in spring they return to the colony areas, taking up their old nest sites or finding new ones close by. Like Adélies, those in the far south have only pebbles and bones for building their nests. Northern gentoos bring in beakfuls of mosses and grasses, trampling and scraping the nests into shape with their big feet.

Their breeding routine is similar to that described for Adélies (page 19). In the far south, gentoos and chinstraps lay a week or two later than Adélies. Northern gentoos may start as much as a month earlier, and tend to take longer over rearing their chicks.

Chinstrap penguins building nest

Gentoo incubating

Chinstrap penguin

Where they live

Chinstrap penguins, like Adélies, swim and catch their food in some of the world's coldest seas, and breed on some of its coldest coasts. However, they are restricted to the Antarctic sector immediately south of South America, including the South Orkney, South Shetland and South Sandwich islands, South Georgia and the Antarctic Peninsula. They do not breed along the coast of mainland Antarctica.

Gentoo penguins share many of the chinstrap breeding areas in the South American sector. They live also on many warmer islands of the southern oceans, including the Falkland Islands in the South Atlantic, the Kerguelen Islands in the southern Indian Ocean, Macquarie Island south of Australia, and several of the island groups south of New Zealand.

ATLANTIC OCEAN
SOUTH GEORGIA
S. SANDWICH IS.
S. ORKNEY IS.
FALKLAND IS.
S. SHETLAND IS.
STATEN I.
ANTARCTIC PENINSULA
INDIAN OCEAN
I. KERGUELEN
HEARD I.
ANTARCTICA
PACIFIC OCEAN
MACQUARIE I.

- ◼ Chinstrap and gentoo penguins
- ◼ Gentoo penguins

VISITING PENGUINS

Up to a few years ago, only explorers and scientists were lucky enough to see Antarctic penguins at home. Today tourists, too, can visit penguin colonies. Some popular colonies are visited almost every day during the season (November to March) by parties of up to 100 tourists at a time. Does it trouble the penguins? Does it affect their breeding or other behaviour?

Scientists who have studied the responses of gentoo penguins to humans say that so long as the tourists, whether alone or in groups, move slowly and remain very quiet, and keep a distance of about 5 m (16 ft) away, the birds seem to accept them and remain untroubled (see also page 43). Incubating birds, which cannot move off without exposing their eggs to cold and predation, seem least bothered by visitors. Even their rate of heartbeat (often an indicator of fear) does not alter when visitors approach, so long as the visitors behave quietly and sensibly.

If you sit quietly on the edge of a colony, very often a gentoo will walk up to you, look you up and down, perhaps peck gently at your boots or clothing. After a time it loses interest and walks away. Impatient tourists try to make the penguins react for their photographs. Sensible ones quickly learn that they get the best photographs by letting the penguins approach them and behave naturally.

Gentoo penguins on a sandy beach

FACT FILE

Family:	Spheniscidae
Latin name:	*Aptenodytes forsteri*
Colour:	Blue-grey head and back, lemon-yellow shirt-front, vivid orange cheek patches, purple bill plates
Standing height:	110 cm (43 in)
Flipper length:	30 cm (12 in)
Weight:	Avge 30 kg (66 lb); up to 41 kg (90 lb)
Breeding range:	Antarctic continent and nearby islands

RELATIONSHIPS

Emperor penguins and king penguins (pages 24-25) are the 'great' penguins, the two biggest species, similar in appearance and closely related to each other. Of the two, emperors are slightly taller and usually very much fatter, with yellow shirt-fronts and narrower bill plates. Their legs are feathered right down to the feet. Both emperors and kings have strangely musical calls, like several notes played simultaneously on reed pipes or an organ.

Some of the other large penguins of the past, known only from fossil bones, were probably close kin to these two species. How closely are emperors and kings related to other kinds of living penguins? Even the experts do not know.

Emperor penguin

King penguin

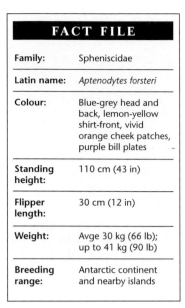

EMPEROR PENGUINS

Majestic golden penguins of the high Antarctic, emperors are the largest of living penguins and the only ones who breed in winter.

EMPERORS ARE the tallest and fattest of all living penguins, with the strangest way of life. They live almost entirely in the cold waters of the Southern Ocean, breeding in colonies close to the Antarctic continent.

There is very little land for emperors to breed on, so they gather in huge colonies on the sea ice that forms every winter in April or May. Sea ice may also be warmer than land. The sea immediately below it is always at −1.8°C (28.8°F), while temperatures on land may fall much lower. Often the colonies gather close to the towering ice cliffs on the coast of Antarctica.

Emperors are unique among penguins in breeding only in winter. They gather in the colonies in April, as soon as the new sea ice is strong enough to bear their weight. Forming pairs, they court with musical, braying calls, by which members of the pair later recognize each other. Each female lays a single egg, usually about mid-May. There is no nest, so the male takes the egg on his feet and holds it against a bare 'brood patch' on his body, under a feathery fold of skin. The females return to sea, usually having to walk several kilometres across the sea ice, leaving the males to incubate for about 64 days.

By mid-July, when the females return to the colonies, the sea ice may be more than 100 km (60 miles) wide. Each female finds her own mate by calling, and takes charge of her egg, which by this time is ready to hatch. Now the males

Adult

Juvenile

leave for the long walk to the open sea, where they dive in and catch their first food for over three months. The females hold the chicks on their feet, and feed them on food brought back in their crops.

After two or three weeks the males return, and then the two parents take turns to feed the chicks. With the sea ice already melting, the birds do not have so far to go. The chicks, covered in thick grey down, grow slowly at first, then more quickly as the rate of feeding increases.

Chick about 3 weeks old on its parent's feet

HUDDLING

To keep warm during winter, when temperatures drop to −40°C (−40°F) and lower, the incubating males huddle tightly together, each with an egg on his feet. They do not leave the colony, so cannot feed. They live instead on their stores of fat, losing weight every day. By the end of incubation their weight may have fallen by half. When the chicks grow too big to fit on their parents' feet, they huddle together in crèches. Their thick grey down helps to keep them warm, but huddling keeps them even warmer.

Chick

FEEDING

Emperor penguins feed mainly on squid, fish and crustaceans, which they catch below the sea ice. Sometimes they dive more than 400 m (1,300 ft) deep. There is little or no light down there, and we do not know how they find their prey. Some of the squid and fish carry tiny lights that the penguins may learn to recognize. Some may make sounds that the penguins can hear, or vibrations that they can feel.

An emperor penguin may travel more than 1,000 km (600 miles) on a single hunting trip, and bring back over 4 kg (9 lb) of food in its crop.

Emperor penguin chasing a squid

KEEPING THEIR COOL

Emperor penguins on land or sea ice are seldom in a hurry. They walk slowly, and in 'toboggan' on their stomachs, pushing themselves along with feet and flippers. If emperors run, they very quickly becomes stressed – out of breath and overheated. This is because of the thickness of fat that they normally carry, and the efficiency of their feathers. Imagine putting on a very thick overcoat and then starting to run – you would soon find yourself getting too hot, and wanting to take your coat off. Emperors cannot take their coats off – they can only stop and cool down.

Where emperors live

There are about 40 known breeding colonies, all very close to the Antarctic continent, with a total population of about 400,000 emperor penguins. Nearly all of the colonies gather on sea ice, which forms when the sea freezes over in winter (usually May or June) and lasts until early summer (usually December or January). Two of the colonies form on small islands surrounded by sea ice. Because they breed in out-of-the- way places and in winter, emperor penguins are difficult to visit. However, tourist parties are flown by helicopter into some of the colonies from ice-breaker ships each year, usually in November or December, so visitors can see and photograph emperor penguins at home.

Emperor penguins

WINTER BREEDING

Emperors breed in winter because they are large birds, with eggs and chicks that take several months to raise. Incubation takes two months, and the chicks take five months to grow. If emperors laid in spring, like other penguins, they would be trying to rear their chicks through the autumn and winter, when the sea ice is most extensive and there is very little food in the sea.

Chicks begin to leave the colonies from late November, usually following the adults over the sea ice towards the open sea. Many at this time are still in down, with their first feathers growing underneath. Though ready for the sea, they weigh only 10–15 kg (22–33 lb), less than half the weight of their parents. By the time they reach the sea most of their down has gone, leaving them in a pale juvenile plumage. They stay in this plumage for a year, then grow full adult plumage, renewing it every year.

The first two or three years of their life are the most dangerous for emperor penguins. Many die in the colonies before they are a year old, and many more during their first and second winters. Those that survive breed for the first time when they are five or six years old, and continue breeding for 20 years or more.

KING PENGUINS

Gold and blue penguins of the Antarctic fringes, even more colourful than their close relatives, the emperors.

FACT FILE	
Family:	Spheniscidae
Latin name:	*Aptenodytes patagonica*
Colour:	Blue-grey head and back, white shirt-front, golden cheek patches, broad orange or purple bill plates
Standing height:	90 cm (35 in)
Flipper length:	29 cm (11 in)
Weight:	Avge 15 kg (33 lb); up to 17 kg (37 lb)
Breeding range:	Cool-temperate islands of the southern oceans

King penguin colony in early summer

RELATIONSHIPS

King penguins are closely related to emperor penguins (pages 22-23), and at first glance look very much like them. However, they are smaller and more slender, with broader orange or purple bill plates. Their flippers are about the same size as an emperor's, so seem to be larger on the smaller, slimmer body. The lower legs are bare of feathers, so kings look as though they are wearing brown leather boots. They live in the cool temperate zone, and seldom stray south into colder water. As a result, the two species are rarely seen together.

Kings are the most colourful and elegant of all the penguins, with blue-grey plumage on the back, flanks and flippers, creamy-white shirt-fronts, black heads and vivid gold patches on either side of the throat. The plates on the lower bill can be any colour from dark blue to salmon pink. A breeding colony of 10,000 kings, closely packed together in courtship and incubation, is an incredible sight. There are dozens of such colonies on islands throughout the southern cool-temperate zone.

King penguins breed on flat raised beaches, usually just a short walk from the sea, often surrounded by coarse tussock grass that protects them from the wind. Breeding starts on the colonies in late spring, about October or early November, though among the newly arriving adults at this time you see hundreds of large brown chicks, with black bills and squeaky, whistling voices. These are the chicks from last season, by this time almost a year old, that have survived winter in the colony.

King penguins, like emperors, are large birds that take a long time to grow. So they too have developed an unusual breeding cycle (see 'Breeding'). They form pairs in spring. Each pair produces a single egg, and rears its chick through the summer. By autumn the chicks are still only three-quarters grown, so they stay in the colonies throughout the winter. By the following spring,

WOOLLY CHICKS

The hunters who first visited the islands of the southern oceans in search of seals discovered groups of strange penguins covered with reddish-brown furry down, like teddy-bears. They killed and skinned some of these strange birds and brought them back to civilization. The museum scientists who described the skins thought they must belong to a new species of penguin, which they called 'woolly penguin'. They turned out, however, to be no more than the chicks of king penguins.

King penguin chick half moulted

when breeding starts again, many 'woolly penguin' chicks from last year remain in the colony, still being fed by their parents.

By mid-November most of the chicks have started to grow feathers, which gradually replace their down. Within two or three weeks they change into slim juveniles, with pale yellow throat patches, and make their way to the sea.

Their parents moult (see page 11), replacing all their feathers, and are soon ready to breed again. However, by this time it is usually too late in the season. They may court, lay an egg and hatch it, but the chick is too small to survive, and dies.

Moulting adults

FEEDING

King penguins feed mainly on small fish, which they catch in depths down to about 300 m (1,000 ft). Occasionally they take squid and shrimps as well. Adults swim up to 30 km (20 miles) from their colonies to forage, bringing back up to 3 kg (6 lb 10oz) of food for their chicks.

BREEDING

The first king penguins to start breeding in spring are usually those that failed to breed in the previous late summer, or lost their chicks during the winter. They moult in September, and return to the colonies to start courting in October.

In courtship, males stand in the colony with head up, neck stretched and flippers extended, making long braying calls that tell females they are ready for mating. Females (which are usually slightly smaller) respond by moving alongside and giving similar calls of their own. Pairs wander off to find a place, often among thousands of others, where they can mate and lay their eggs without too much jostling and fighting with others. The first eggs appear in late November.

There is no nest. Like emperors, kings carry the egg on their feet, pressed against a bare patch on their abdomen for warmth, and protected by surrounding feathers. The males take charge of the eggs, and incubate them on their feet for the first two or three weeks, while the females return to the sea and feed. Then the females return, and the two partners take turns at incubating. The eggs hatch after 54 days, and the brown downy chicks are fed by both parents from their crops. They grow quickly, and by April have reached weights of about 10 kg (22 lb).

Where kings live

King penguins breed on most of the islands in the southern cool-temperate zone, including the Falklands, South Georgia, Marion, Crozet, Kerguelen, Heard and Macquarie islands. Hunted for oil during the 1800s, they were exterminated altogether from some of these areas and severely reduced on others, but seem now to be increasing rapidly on most or all of their breeding grounds.

WINTERING CHICKS

During winter the weather in the breeding colonies grows colder and more windy, and snow covers the ground. The amount of food available in the southern oceans decreases sharply, and many kinds of animals go hungry. King penguin chicks that have been fed regularly every two or three days through late summer and autumn, reaching weights of 10 kg (22 lb) or more, find feeding visits severely reduced from late April. They may now see their parents only once every three or four weeks.

All the unoccupied adults leave the colony for the winter. The chicks huddle together – several thousand of them in a single mass – to keep warm. When a parent returns to the colony with food, it stands at the edge of the huddle and calls. If its own chick hears, the chick responds with a whistling call of its own. Parent and chick recognize each other by their calls. The two get together, and the chick is fed for two or three days.

During these hard winter months, not surprisingly, every chick loses weight. Those that start the winter at only 5–6 kg (11–13 lb) have little chance of surviving the lean months. They starve to death. Those that start at 10 kg (22 lb) or more stand a better chance. Living mainly on their fat, they survive until September, when food returns to the sea and feeding visits become more frequent. By October the survivors are fattening again. By November they weigh almost as much as their parents, and are starting to shed their down.

ROCKHOPPER PENGUINS

Gold-crested clowns of the Antarctic fringe.

FACT FILE

Family:	Spheniscidae
Latin name:	*Eudyptes chrysocome*
Colour:	Black head and back, white shirt-front, golden-yellow and black crests on forehead, brown bill, red eyes
Standing height:	47 cm (19 in)
Flipper length:	15.3 cm (6 in)
Weight:	Avge 2.4 kg (5 lb); up to 4.2 kg (11 lb)
Breeding range:	Cool-temperate islands of the southern oceans

RELATIONSHIPS

Eudyptes, meaning 'beautiful' diver, is the generic name of six kinds of penguin, all similar in appearance and closely related to each other. This species, whose specific name *chrysocome* means 'golden-haired', is the smallest and neatest of the six, with the reddest eyes, the sharpest bill and the widest geographical range. Its golden eyebrow plumes, narrow above the eyes, flare out and droop behind. There are three subspecies, closely similar but with slightly different lengths and arrangements of their golden eyebrow plumes.

THE WESTERN ISLANDS of the Falklands are wild and stormy. Towering cliffs line the coast, cut by steep gullies and pounded by waves that fling spray high into the air. Those cliffs and rough seas are the home of thousands of rockhoppers − small crested penguins that spend most of their lives in the water but come ashore for four months each year to build nests, lay eggs and rear their chicks.

On land their home is a flat rocky plain at the top of a gully, over 100 m (300 ft) above the sea. Though well out of reach of the waves, it is windy and rainswept, offering little shelter or comfort. The gully, strewn with boulders, is a long climb for small birds with short legs, particularly when they are bringing home a cropful of food − perhaps the second or third in a day − for a hungry chick.

To get ashore, the penguins land on a rocky ledge and scramble upwards between waves. Often they are washed off. They have to try again and again before landing safely.

Rockhoppers are so named because they hop. They are not the only penguins that hop, but they hop more than any others, perhaps because of their size and the rocky ground.

Moulting rockhopper penguins

FEEDING

Rockhoppers feed mainly on crustaceans and small fish, which they catch in surface waters. Though able to dive to 100 m (300 ft) or more, they seem to catch most of their food close to the surface, sometimes travelling long distances from land. Their crops are small, so they can bring back only 200–300 g (7–10 oz) of food at a time for their chicks.

This rockhopper belongs to the subspecies with the longest plumes

BREEDING

Rockhoppers nest in numbers ranging from small groups of a dozen or so to colonies of several thousand. They are absent from the colonies in winter, returning from September onwards to breed. They are sturdy fighters, battling with bills and flippers for nesting space in the big colonies. During courtship they call and shake their heads violently, making their crests swirl like golden flowers.

Like all other crested penguins, rockhoppers lay two eggs, the first slightly smaller than the second. The first is usually lost from the nest before incubation starts, and snapped up by skuas or other predators. The second egg is closely guarded and incubated, first by the female, later by the two parents in turn, for a total of about 34 days. The chicks, with brown backs and white fronts, take about five weeks to reach nearly full-size, and a further three or four weeks before they moult into juvenile plumage.

EGGS OF DIFFERENT SIZES

Birds that lay two or more eggs usually make them of similar size. Most penguins lay eggs that differ in weight by only 5% or less. The crested penguins lay two eggs, but of quite different sizes.

The difference is greatest in erect-crested penguins (pages 30–31), in which the smaller first egg is only about half as big as the larger. It is least in fiordland penguins, the little egg being about one-fifth smaller. In rockhoppers, the smaller egg is about two-thirds the size of the larger one.

The first egg is nearly always lost before incubation starts, so only one chick is raised. Occasionally both eggs survive, producing one small and one larger chick. When this happens, the larger chick usually gets most of the food, and the smaller one dies. If the larger chick is lost, the smaller becomes the sole survivor. Either way, only one chick survives.

Biologists are puzzled by this curious business. Laying two eggs but producing only one chick seems a waste of food and energy. The most likely explanation is that, for some reason (perhaps because of their small crop), crested penguins cannot normally raise two chicks, even though they lay two eggs. Rather than putting all their efforts into one big egg (remember, they are small birds), they divide them among two, but unevenly. They lay a small egg that might survive, and a larger one that almost certainly will. The first is an insurance, in case the second is damaged or broken.

Rockhopper incubating a single large egg

Where rockhoppers live

Rockhopper penguins range widely over the islands of the southern oceans. The subspecies with the shortest plumes breeds only on the Falklands Islands and some islands close to Cape Horn. The subspecies with the medium-sized plumes breeds on Marion, Crozet, Kerguelen, Heard and Macquarie islands (shown here on the map) and on Campbell Island and the Auckland and Antipodes groups (see map on page 31). The subspecies with the longest plumes breeds mainly on warmer islands in the Atlantic and Indian oceans..

There are probably more than 2.5 million pairs of rockhoppers on the Falklands, and almost 1 million on other cool-temperate islands. Of the long-crested subspecies, only a few thousand pairs remain.

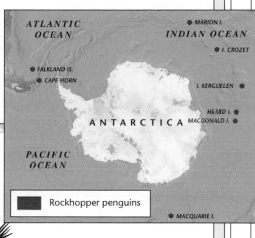

Rockhopper hopping

HOPPING

Once they are on land rockhopper penguins start to hop. With head forward, both feet together, tail up and flippers outstretched for balance, they hop from boulder to boulder. They hold on with their sharp claws, occasionally grasping, digging-in or steadying themselves with their sharp, pointed bill.

HOW THE FIRST EGG DISAPPEARS

In any of the penguins that build nests, one partner, usually the female, sits in the nest while the other brings stones, sticks or clumps of moss and places them within reach. The sitting bird pulls the material in, at the same time shaping the nest bowl by scraping it with her feet.

In most species, the scraping behaviour stops before the first egg is laid. In crested penguins, scraping continues after the first egg appears. Almost inevitably, the bird scrapes the egg out of the nest. Once it has rolled away, it is of no further interest to either partner. So it makes a meal for a predatory skua or gull.

Nesting rockhoppers

FACT FILE

MACARONI PENGUIN

Family:	Spheniscidae
Latin name:	*Eudyptes chrysolophus*
Colour:	Black head, face, throat and back, white shirt-front, orange-yellow crests that meet above the eyes
Standing height:	60 cm (24 in)
Flipper length:	20 cm (8 in)
Weight:	Avge 4.6 kg (10 lb); up to 6.9 kg (15 lb)
Breeding range:	Cool-temperate and Antarctic fringe islands

ROYAL PENGUIN

Family:	Spheniscidae
Latin name:	*Eudyptes schlegeli*
Colour:	Black head and back, white or mottled grey face and throat, white shirt-front, orange-yellow and black crests that meet above the eyes
Standing height:	60 cm (24 in)
Flipper length:	19 cm (7 in)
Weight:	Avge 4.9 kg (11 lb); up to 8.1 kg (18 lb)
Breeding range:	Macquarie Island

MACARONI AND ROYAL PENGUINS

Gold-crested penguins of the sub-Antarctic.

MACARONI AND ROYAL penguins are plentiful in the cool temperate and cold regions of the southern oceans, though with different distributions. Larger and heavier than rockhoppers, and with a different arrangement of orange-gold plumes, they walk rather than hop. However, they are no less able to scramble over rocks and climb steep slopes to reach their nests.

Both at sea and on land they are highly social. Typically they breed in huge colonies numbering tens or hundreds of thousands. After breeding, at the end of autumn, they leave their colonies altogether and spend their winters at sea.

We do not know where they go, but sometimes there are reports of large groups swimming together, usually in warmer waters to the north of their breeding areas. Macaroni penguins occasionally appear on the beaches of South America and South Africa, royal penguins in Australia and New Zealand.

Royal penguin and chick

WHY MACARONI AND ROYAL?

The travellers who first saw macaroni penguins were reminded of young gentlemen in London who, in the fashion of the time, wore gaudy hats with feathers. Londoners called these dandies 'macaronis' – probably because they had brought the fashion back from travels in Italy. So the penguins with brilliant crests became macaroni penguins. Similarly, any particularly colourful or splendid animal or plant was called 'royal', and someone thought that these penguins with the very impressive crests deserved the name.

FEEDING

Macaroni penguins feed almost entirely on crustaceans, which they catch near the surface. Also included in their diet are small fish and squid. Those that live on Heard Island, in the southern Indian Ocean, seem to catch more fish, though still relying heavily on crustaceans. Royal penguins also eat crustaceans, fish and squid, but fish make up a higher proportion, usually at least half, of their diet. Both species may travel over 30 km (20 miles) for their food and can carry 600 g (20 oz) or more of food in their crops.

RELATIONSHIPS

These two closely related species of crested penguins are very similar – enough for some biologists to include them in a single species. Macaroni penguins are widespread across the cool southern oceans, breeding as far south as the fringes of Antarctica. Within that range they show very little variation. Royal penguins breed on only one island, Macquarie Island, in the cold waters south of Tasmania.

Macaroni penguin

To look at, the differences between them are slight. They are similar in size and weight, though royals may at times be slightly heavier. The plumes of both start from a central point on the forehead, like hair parted down the middle. They include both orange and yellow feathers. Macaronis typically have a black face and throat. In royals the face is white or grey, the throat white. Both species have a small white patch at the base of the tail.

Royal penguin

Macaroni penguin

Where they live

Macaronis are one of the commoner penguin species, with a total population estimated at about 12 million pairs. South Georgia alone is home to about 5 million pairs. Over 2 million pairs breed on the Crozet Islands, almost 2 million on the Kerguelen Islands, over 1 million on Heard Island, 1 million on the Macdonald Islands and half a million on Marion Island. They breed also on the Falkland Islands, in southern Chile, on the South Shetland, South Orkney and South Sandwich islands.

Royal penguins in contrast breed only on Macquarie Island, where there are about 850,000 pairs.

■ Macaroni penguins
▨ Royal penguins

BREEDING

Both macaroni and royal penguins spend the four or five winter months at sea, returning to their colonies between mid-September and October. The colonies are usually on flat ground near the sea. Males are first to return, and first to take up their nest sites in the colonies, often finding the exact site where they nested in the previous year. Females also head for their old site. If their previous partner is already there, they are likely to pair up again. If not, or if either is delayed, they find other partners among neighbours, or among young birds entering the colony to breed for the first time.

Royal penguins start laying during the second week in October, and by the end of the month nearly all have an egg. Macaronis breed slightly later, usually in November. In both, two eggs are laid, the first about two-thirds the size of the second. The first egg almost always disappears. Parents share the incubation, which takes 35 days, and both feed the single chicks, which take nine to ten weeks to grow, moult, and leave the colonies for the sea.

NAVIGATION

How do penguins find their way around? The oceans are huge, their island homes relatively small. Yet a royal penguin hatched and raised on Macquarie Island can leave it as a juvenile, wander the ocean for several months, and then find its way back – not only to the island, but to the colony where it was raised. Later, as a breeding bird, it will return each year, making many long journeys in search of food, returning each time to the same nest to feed its chick.

Most birds navigate by the sun – though exactly how is not known. When we navigate by the sun, we need good weather to see it clearly, a sextant to measure its height above the horizon, a chronometer to tell accurate time and a book of navigational tables. Penguins manage without any of these, often during long spells of cloudy weather when it is hard to see the sun at all. There is something here that we might learn from them – if we knew how.

Macaroni penguins travel widely, but return to breed in the same nest

FACT FILE

ERECT-CRESTED PENGUIN

Family:	Spheniscidae
Latin name:	*Eudyptes sclateri*
Colour:	Black head and back, white shirt-front, cheeks black, broad yellow brushlike crests extending from either side of the bill over the eyes
Standing height:	57 cm (22 in)
Flipper length:	18 cm (7 in)
Weight:	Avge 4.5 kg (10 lb); up to 6.3 kg (14 lb)
Breeding range:	Antipodes, Bounty and Auckland islands

FIORDLAND PENGUIN

Family:	Spheniscidae
Latin name:	*Eudyptes pachyrhynchus*
Colour:	Black head and back, white shirt-front, cheeks black with white streaks, broad yellow crests extending from either side of the bill over the eyes, flaring at back of the head
Standing height:	47 cm (19 in)
Flipper length:	16 cm (6 in)
Weight:	Avge 4 kg (9 lb); up to 5.2 kg (11 lb)
Breeding range:	Southwest coast of South Island and Stewart Island, New Zealand

SNARES PENGUIN

Family:	Spheniscidae
Latin name:	*Eudyptes robustus*
Colour:	Black head and back, white shirt-front, black cheeks, white or pink skin at base of bill, broad yellow crests extending from either side of the bill over the eyes
Standing height:	47 cm (19 in)
Flipper length:	16 cm (6 in)
Weight:	Avge 3.8 kg (8 lb); up to 4.3 kg (9 lb)
Breeding range:	Snares Islands

MORE CRESTED PENGUINS

Erect-crested, Fiordland and Snares penguins from southern New Zealand and islands farther south.

Meeting these three species of crested penguins in a zoo, you would find them hard to tell apart. You could not mistake them for macaroni or royal penguins, because the gleaming yellow crests do not meet in the middle. You might mistake them for rockhoppers, but they are bigger and more chunky, with thicker, heavier bills.

These are the main differences between the three species. Erect-crested penguins are some 10 cm (4 in) taller than the other two. Fiordland penguins have prominent white streaks on the cheeks that nearly always show when they are awake and active. Snares penguins have a narrow strip of pink or white flesh at the angle of the bill, extending along the lower half of the bill. All three look rather alike when their crests are sleeked down. When they raise them, erect-crested penguins look as though they are wearing two rows of yellow bristles, quite different in texture from the softer plumes of the other two species.

On the breeding grounds they are much easier to separate. Though any of them may breed away from their normal areas, very few of them seem to do so. On the Snares Islands, with very few exceptions, you see only Snares penguins, in Fiordland only the Fiordland penguin, and on Antipodes Island and the Bounties only erect-crested penguins.

Fiordland penguins at home on the coast of New Zealand

BREEDING

Like other crested penguins, all three species leave the breeding areas in autumn, and remain at sea for several months. Fiordland penguins are the first to return, appearing on the nesting grounds in June and July. By early August most of them have nests and are already incubating. Snares penguins return to their islands one to two months later, in August and early September, and lay between mid-September and mid-October. Erect-crested penguins return two to three weeks later still, laying in late October and early November. In each species, breeding pairs lay two eggs but incubate only one, raising a single chick.

FEEDING

All three New Zealand species are believed to feed on shrimp-like crustaceans, probably also on small fish and squid, which they catch close to the surface, and probably within easy swimming distance of the breeding colonies.

Snares penguin

RELATIONSHIPS

These three kinds of crested penguins, all closely related, are confusingly similar when you see them in the field. All live in southern New Zealand or on islands farther south. Erect-crested penguins are slightly larger and heavier than the others. Although they wander into each other's areas, especially in winter when they are away from home, they breed in quite different places, and at different times of year.

Erect-crested penguin

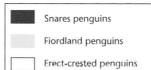

Fiordland penguin

SPECIES OR SUBSPECIES?

Members of a species breed only with their own kind. Although the three penguins on this page live close to each other and are very similar, they do not breed together. This is why biologists treat them as different species. If a species has two or more distinct populations, breeding in different areas, the members of each population may come to look slightly different, although they can still breed with each other. Each population is then called a subspecies. If they remain separated, they may eventually be unable to breed with each other, like the three types of crested penguins here.

Where they live

Fiordland penguins are the most easily accessible of the three species. They live around the densely forested coasts of southwestern New Zealand. Coastal roads have penetrated Fiordland, and the penguins can be found in cavities under fallen logs, among roots and tangled undergrowth, in rocky caverns and caves, usually within a few metres of the sea. You find them also on Stewart Island, mostly in the wildest areas away from settlements.

To find Snares penguins, people must take a fishing boat from Stewart Island for a four-hour voyage south. The islands are tree-covered and overgrown, and visitors must have a permit. You can see the penguins in the water and lining the rocky shores, and may even glimpse one of their colonies among the trees just inshore.

Meeting erect-crested penguins involves a longer journey by sea.

The nearest colonies are on the Auckland Islands, 560 km (350 miles) south of New Zealand, where large numbers nest among tussock grass and wind-carved trees. This is one of the very few places where penguins and parrots can be seen nesting side by side. They live also on the Bounty Islands, a group of bare granitic rocks about 1,000 km (625 miles) to the east, and the nearby Antipodes Islands.

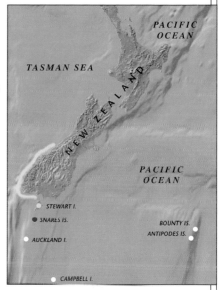

Snares penguins
Fiordland penguins
Erect-crested penguins

HOW MANY ARE THERE?

We do not know how many Fiordland penguins there are. They nest in secret, widely scattered colonies, making it difficult even to estimate their numbers. Some biologists think there are 5,000 or more pairs, others as few as 1,000 pairs. All agree that numbers are declining. This may be a species in need of protection (see pages 42-43).

Snares penguins are easier to see and count. The four main islands of the group, which are small enough to examine fairly thoroughly, support at least 23,000 pairs. Erect-crested penguins, also relatively easy to count, are far more plentiful. Antipodes Island and the Bounty Islands each support 100,000 pairs or more.

YELLOW-EYED PENGUINS

Shy penguins of southeastern New Zealand.

FACT FILE	
Family:	Spheniscidae
Latin name:	*Megadyptes antipodes*
Colour:	Back blue-back, head brown with yellow-and-black cheeks and coronet, yellow band across crown, yellow eyes
Standing height:	60 cm (24 in)
Flipper length:	19 cm (7 in)
Weight:	Avge 5.5 kg (12 lb); up to 9 kg (20 lb)
Breeding range:	Southeastern New Zealand, Auckland Islands, Campbell Island

Yellow-eyed penguins courting

RELATIONSHIPS

The yellow-eyed penguin is quite different from other species. Its Latin name means 'large diver of the Antipodes' — it is the third-largest penguin, after emperors and kings, and 'Antipodes' was the name given to the part of the world farthest from Europe. In a genus of their own, yellow-eyed penguins have no obvious close relations among the rest of the penguins. The curious head markings and yellow, cat-like eyes are unique. Their behaviour, too, is different. While most other penguins nest in huge colonies and never like to be alone, these are shy, solitary birds that nest apart from each other. They seldom meet even on the beaches.

To MEET YELLOW-EYED penguins you have to visit southern New Zealand or some of its neighbouring islands. You need to know where to find them, for yellow-eyed penguins nest in out-of-the-way places along steep, rugged shores, in caverns and in holes among dense flax or tussock grass.

Local people know where they live. Visitors may need a permit or guide, because there are not many yellow-eyed penguins left. Most of their breeding grounds are on private property or reserves, and those who care for them guard them closely.

The best chance of seeing them is in the early mornings, when they leave the colonies and walk down to the sea, and in the evenings when they return. They can be seen on the beaches, and often leave their footprints along the muddy cliff paths. In spring the calls that form part of their courtship chuckling, grunting and loud, full-throated yelling and trumpeting can be clearly heard.

Walking slowly and quietly along their paths, visitors may see them standing alongside their nests, or sleeping in the sunshine. If they see or hear people coming, they will disappear quickly around the corner.

BREEDING

Pairs form in August and September, usually well away from other nests, and in a place where one or other has nested before. Defending their territory against intruders with threat displays and calls, each pair finds a sheltered corner, perhaps under an overhanging tussock, where they gather a nest of sticks, grass and moss. They mate in September, producing two white eggs which they take turns to incubate.

The chicks, in overall down hatch after about 45 days. Both parents feed them, and in normal years they grow rapidly, by late February reaching or even exceeding the weight of an adult. In some years food is scarce, slowing their growth. If it is very scarce, one or both of them may starve to death.

Yellow-eyed penguin and chicks on nesting ground

The family group depicted below left consists of two chicks (left) and an adult, close to their nest among the flax and tussock grass. This is a busy time for the parents, for the chicks are growing fast, and always hungry. Though one or other parent stayed on guard when they were younger, the chicks are now big enough to be left on their own, so both parents can fish at the same time. One has brought back two or three kilograms of small fish. The other will bring in another cropful for the evening meal. Sadly, all these penguins are in danger from introduced predators. If a ferret, stoat or wild cat finds them, both chicks and adults may be killed.

Resting in the sunshine

A LONG STUDY

For 18 years, between 1936 and 1954, Lancelot Richdale, a New Zealand teacher and naturalist, used his spare time to study the yellow-eyed penguins of Otago Peninsula, close to his home city of Dunedin. By banding several hundred birds (see page 43), he came to know them as individuals. Turning out in all weathers and spending many hours watching them, he discovered details of their breeding behaviour, partnerships, courting, nesting, family relationships, how long they lived and many other facts about their lives.

Towards the end of his observations, Richdale was studying the children and grandchildren of some of his earliest banded birds. This was the first-ever long-term study of banded penguins, and is still one of the best.

FEEDING

Yellow-eyed penguins feed mainly on small fish and squid, which they catch in shallow coastal waters, mostly within 24 km (15 miles) of the shore. They can dive to 50 m (165 ft) or more, but find most of their food near the surface. A full crop contains over 3.5 kg (8 lb) of food.

Where they live

Yellow-eyed penguins breed along the coast of Southland and Otago, on New Zealand's South Island, and also on Stewart Island, the Auckland Islands and Campbell Island, immediately south of New Zealand. These are all small, scattered populations, each numbering only 300-400 pairs. The total world population of yellow-eyed penguins is only about 5,000 individuals.

You seldom see them anywhere except close to their breeding grounds. Occasionally one or two – usually young birds – are spotted as far north as Cook Strait, between New Zealand's North and South islands.

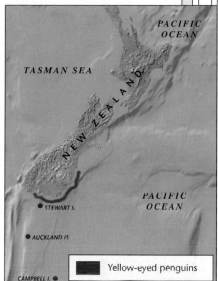

Yellow-eyed penguins

WHERE HAVE THEY GONE?

There were probably more yellow-eyed penguins along New Zealand's coasts in the past. Until about AD 950, New Zealand had no human population. Its first settlers were Polynesian hunters who made room for their villages by burning areas of forest. They would have met yellow-eyed penguins, taken them for food and perhaps destroyed some of their habitat, though only on a small scale.

European settlers from the late 1700s onwards burnt more of the coastal forests and grasslands for farming. We do not know how many yellow-eyed penguins nested on the South Island before the Europeans arrived, but the new settlers' cattle and sheep browsed the vegetation and trod on nesting sites. Their cats and dogs, and the stoats and ferrets that they introduced, took penguins and chicks at the nests. Commercial fishermen competed with the penguins for food, and their nets caught penguins in the water.

Numbers of yellow-eyed penguins have continued to fall on both the mainland and the islands, even during the last 40 years when many of their breeding grounds have been protected. Mainland breeding grounds are still harried by cats and other predators. Island stocks are seldom visited, but commercial fishing may still compete with them for food. New Zealand biologists are concerned for the future of their yellow-eyed penguins.

JACKASS PENGUINS

Burrowing penguins of the sandy beaches of Namibia and South Africa, protected by the locals but in constant danger.

FACT FILE

Family:	Spheniscidae
Latin name:	*Spheniscus demersus*
Colour:	Black head, back, cheeks and chin; white bars on sides of head joining across throat; white shirt-front with black transverse bar across the chest and scattered black spots; pink and black feet
Standing height:	60 cm (24 in)
Flipper length:	16.5 cm (6 in)
Weight:	Avge 3.5 kg (8 lb); up to 4.9 kg (11 lb)
Breeding range:	Southwest and southern coasts of South Africa

SPECIES IN DANGER

South Africa and Namibia still have plenty of wilderness coasts and islands, particularly in the southwestern desert areas, where people and domestic animals are few. There jackass penguins continue their own way of life. However, several islands have been devastated in the past by the collection of guano – sea-bird droppings, valued as a fertilizer for agriculture (see page 39). In addition, commercial fishing offshore competes with the penguins for food. And there is a constant danger of oil spills and leakage from ships passing along the coast. Hundreds of penguins die each year from this cause, and a bad spill or wreck close to one of the larger breeding grounds is capable of destroying many thousands at once. So, although there are tens of thousands of jackass penguins in the world, South African biologists regard this as a species in danger, and keep a very close eye on its welfare.

Nesting among rocks and vegetation

JACKASS PENGUINS may be seen along many sandy beaches in southern Africa. Their favourite haunts are sheltered bays, with boulders that offer shade from the sun, and a background of stable sand dunes covered with vegetation, where they can nest. There they live the year round, with plenty of food in the cool waters just offshore, and a permanent home – perhaps more than one – in a burrow or under a bush just a few metres' walk inland.

Unfortunately for the penguins, southern South Africa has become heavily populated with humans, who like to live in just the same kind of bays, and build their homes along the coast. Where the settlers have taken over, lining the coast with cities, roads, railways, docks and quays, the penguins have given up and left. But where there are still open beaches with relatively unspoiled country beyond, the penguins are still there, continuing their age-old ways of life.

These were probably the first-ever penguins seen by European explorers. An expedition led by the Portuguese explorer Bartolomeu Dias discovered and rounded the southern tip of Africa in 1487–88. There are no records of penguins from that voyage, but a later expedition, led by Vasco da Gama, found flightless birds as big as ducks on an island in one of the bays. Starved of fresh meat, they killed and ate them.

Jackass penguins today seem happy to share their beaches with bathers, kite-flyers and sand-castle builders, and continue to dig their burrows in gardens and parks beyond. Local people in turn protect the penguins, providing walkways from the beaches, teaching schoolchildren to care for them and fencing off nesting areas to keep dogs and cattle away.

RELATIONSHIPS

Jackass penguins, also called African or black-footed penguins, are one of four species in the genus *Spheniscus*, a name meaning 'wedge-shaped'. Called the 'burrowing penguins', spheniscids nest underground in burrows they have dug for themselves or stolen from each other. Jackass penguins get their species name *demersus* from a Latin word meaning 'underwater'. Why 'jackass'? Because, during the breeding season, they attract mates by braying like donkeys.

BREEDING

In wilderness areas, jackass penguins nest in large colonies on rough, stony ground, often under trees or shrubs, or in burrows where the ground is soft enough to dig. Among human settlements, they form smaller, scattered colonies, sometimes nesting under houses or garden sheds. They breed throughout the year, each colony showing peaks of laying in different months. Each pair produces two eggs, the first slightly smaller than the second. Both parents incubate in turn for a total of 38 days,

Preening after a swim

FEEDING

Jackass penguins feed chiefly on small fish, which they catch mainly at or close to the surface, usually within 120 km (75 miles) of their breeding grounds. Some of the species are caught by commercial fishing vessels too, so penguins and fishermen compete. They also eat shrimps and squid, though in smaller quantities.

Panting in strong sunshine

then tend the chicks for a further 10-19 weeks. If all goes well they raise two chicks successfully, but there are many dangers on the way. Rainstorms and flooding may drown whole colonies. Gulls, ibises and other birds prey constantly on the nests. And seasonal scarcity of fish may starve many chicks to death.

Where jackasses live

Jackass penguins live on near-shore islands and mainland coasts of southern Africa, from Namibia in the west to South Africa along the south. Within this wide span there are many scattered colonies, making it difficult to estimate numbers. There may be as many as 150,000 breeding pairs, or as few as 50,000. Numbers seem in any case to fluctuate widely, as breeding success varies from colony to colony and from year to year.

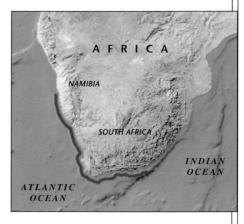

AFRICA

NAMIBIA

SOUTH AFRICA

INDIAN OCEAN

ATLANTIC OCEAN

■ Jackass penguins

BURROWING

Rabbits, dogs, badgers and ferrets burrow by digging with their front feet and claws. A penguin's flippers are the wrong shape for digging and too easily damaged. Instead, the penguin finds a ledge or hump in the ground, sometimes the root of a grassy tussock, and starts to dig with its bill, biting out chunks of earth and throwing them over its shoulder. Then it turns sideways and scrapes with its feet to move the loose earth, then digs again with its bill. In soft turf or sandy soil it can make good headway, burrowing its own length in less than an hour. Within two

or three hours it is well underground, still digging furiously with its bill, and pushing the soil back with its feet to make a mound at the burrow entrance. Eventually the burrow may be 2 m (over 6 ft) long and 1 m (over 3 ft) below ground, with a round nesting chamber at the end.

But, as every penguin knows, it is easier to take over a ready-made burrow. Some are lucky enough to find an abandoned burrow. Some displace another penguin from a burrow, or even move in to share with another penguin.

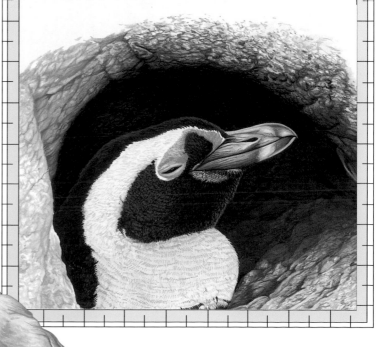

FACT FILE

Family:	Spheniscidae
Latin name:	*Spheniscus magellanicus*
Colour:	Black head, back, cheeks and chin, white bars on sides of head joining across throat, white shirt-front with two black transverse bars across the upper part of the chest, pink and black feet
Standing height:	60 cm (24 in)
Flipper length:	17 cm (7 in)
Weight:	Avge 4.5 kg (10 lb); up to 7.8 kg (17 lb)
Breeding range:	Falkland Islands, southern South America

Magellanic penguin chick

RELATIONSHIPS

These are burrowing penguins of southern Argentina and Chile, closely related to the Peruvian and Galapagos penguins that live to the north of them along the coasts of Chile and Peru (pages 38-39), and to jackass penguins of southern Africa (pages 34-35). They differ from jackasses and Peruvian penguins by having two bars of black feathers across the shirt-front, the upper like a collar across the throat, the lower extending down either flank almost to the feet. Galapagos penguins similarly have two dark bands, Peruvians only one.

MAGELLANIC PENGUINS

Burrowing penguins of the Falkland Islands and South America.

MAGELLANIC PENGUINS seem equally at home on the desert coasts of Argentina, the cooler sandy shores of the Falkland Islands and the forested fiords of southern Chile. Typical breeding grounds are broad, flat areas of sand, gravel and clay, which are scattered with shrubs or tall grasses that provide shelter from the wind and shade from the sun. But they also breed in dense forests of southern beech and stands of tussock grass, where their nests are linked by muddy pathways leading to the sea.

The name Magellanic comes from the Portuguese navigator Ferdinand Magellan, whose round-the-world expedition of 1519 to 1522 first explored the coasts where they live. On islands along the shore of what is now Patagonia (in southern Argentina), his crewmen became the first Europeans to meet South American penguins. The men thought these strange birds must be some kind of flightless geese, and were interested only in eating them.

Magellanic penguins stand as tall as jackass penguins, but are usually fatter and chunkier. On the Falkland Islands they often share beaches with gentoo penguins, where they show an interesting difference. Even from a distance you can spot Magellanics by the way they stand and walk. Gentoos, like most other penguins, stand upright and strut with their flippers held out sideways. Magellanics, like the rest of the burrowing penguins, often bend forward and trot, with flippers in front. When they are in a hurry, they scuttle on all fours.

FEEDING

Magellanic penguins feed mainly on small fish, which swarm in enormous schools off their breeding grounds during spring and summer. They also eat squid and crustaceans, but fish are more reliable and are their mainstay throughout the year. They have been known to dive to 90 m (300 ft) or more, but most of their food lives within 30 m (100 ft) of the surface, and that is where they hunt most. Parents can carry up to 400 g (14 oz) of food in their crops for hungry chicks.

BREEDING

Between May and August, Magellanic penguins are at sea, leaving the breeding grounds deserted. They return in September, taking over and refurbishing old nest sites, digging new burrows and reshaping old ones. By late October they have paired, and most are already incubating two white eggs. Incubation takes about 41 days, with both parents sharing. Chicks remain closely brooded in the nests for three to four weeks, then are left on their own while both parents seek food at sea. Fully grown at 12 weeks, they moult into juvenile plumage and leave, usually between January and March. Relieved of their duties, the parents also moult into fresh new feathers, and leave in April or May for their long winter vacation.

PENGUINS, SEA LIONS AND KILLER WHALES

Over most of their range, Magellanic penguins share beaches with thousands of sea lions, which breed in huge mobs close to the sea during the summer and are present in all but the winter months. Sea lions feed mostly on squid and fish, which they hunt in deep waters offshore. In the shallows closer to home they meet and mix with penguins, which they sometimes chase, grab and throw into the air. Only rarely do they eat them. Chasing may be fun for the sea lions, but not for the penguins. On the beaches you see damaged and torn penguins, and dead ones with cut skin and flippers.

Off southern Patagonia, killer whales do exactly the same to the sea lions, chasing them, sometimes throwing them up and catching them. However, this is predation rather than play. It usually ends with the whale eating the sea lion. Killer whales probably eat penguins too, but it must take several dozen to make a square meal for even a small whale.

Magellanic penguins entering the water

Where Magellanics live

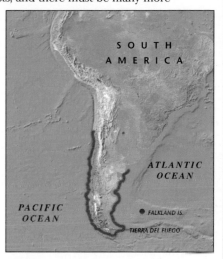

Magellanic penguins breed on the Atlantic coast of South America as far north as San Matias Gulf, off Argentina, and on the Pacific coast to Talcahuano, Chile. They breed also on the Falkland Islands, scattered along the shores of the two main islands and dozens of smaller tussock-covered islands. Argentina has over 20 known colonies, some with several thousand nests, and there must be many more colonies unknown and uncounted in the wilds of Tierra del Fuego and southern Chile. The Falkland Islands support over 90 small colonies. We do not know the total population of Magellanic penguins, but it is likely to exceed 1 million pairs.

■ Magellanic penguins

CAPE HORN

Cape Horn stands on a small island just south of Tierra del Fuego. The Cape itself is a steep cliff of brown rock, 424 m (1,391 ft) high, facing south over one of the world's stormiest patches of ocean. The north side of the island has gentler slopes, covered with tussock grass over 1 m (3 ft 3 in) tall. Among the tussock grasses live hundreds of Magellanic penguins in a city of well-hidden nests.

The winds howl around Cape Horn, the oceans roar and tumble. In times past this was the graveyard of hundreds of sailing ships. For the penguins, storms and rough seas are no problem. However strong the wind, on land the tussock grass protects them. Under it, they go quietly about their business of nesting and rearing chicks. Though waves 20 m (66 ft) high beat against the south face of the island, on the north side they have their own sheltered harbour. The rougher the ocean, the richer it is, providing more food for penguins and thousands of other hungry sea-birds.

Penguin in its burrow

PERUVIAN AND GALAPAGOS PENGUINS

Burrowing penguins of tropical South America.

FACT FILE

PERUVIAN PENGUIN

Family:	Spheniscidae
Latin name:	*Spheniscus humboldti*
Colour:	Black head, cheeks and chin, dark brownish-black back, extensive bare skin around base of the bill, broad white bars on sides of head joining across throat, white shirt-front with single black bar, and a few scattered black spots
Standing height:	55 cm (22 in)
Flipper length:	17 cm (7 in)
Weight:	Avge 4.7 kg (10 lb); up to 5.8 kg (13 lb)
Breeding range:	Coast of northern Chile and Peru

GALAPAGOS PENGUIN

Family:	Spheniscidae
Latin name:	*Spheniscus mendiculus*
Colour:	Grey-black head, cheeks and chin, dark grey-black back, bare pink skin around base of bill, narrow white bars on sides of head joining across throat, white shirt-front with two dark bars across it
Standing height:	45 cm (18 in)
Flipper length:	13 cm (5 in)
Weight:	Avge 2.3 kg (5 lb); up to 3.5 kg (8 lb)
Breeding range:	Fernandina and Isabela islands of the Galapagos Islands

BREEDING

Peruvian penguins are present in their colonies all the year round, and breeding pairs can be found in any month. They lay two white eggs, sharing the incubation of about 40 days. Chicks take about 12 weeks to mature. Galapagos penguins, too, breed at any time of the year, successful nests raising two chicks.

PERUVIAN PENGUINS are at home on the desert coasts of northern Chile and Peru, sharing islands and stretches of mainland coast with thousands of flying sea-birds. Most of them breed in colonies on offshore islands. Some survive on headlands and rocky parts of the coast, where they may be raided by foxes, dogs and other predators. They nest in caves, under rocks and sparse shrubs, and in burrows, usually in groups of a dozen or more pairs. There are also larger colonies, numbering hundreds of pairs. Very little remains of the guano (see opposite page) in which they used to burrow, and only in a few places is the soil deep enough for safe underground homes. Years of human predation have made them wary and secretive when people are around.

Galapagos penguins breed on two or possibly more of the Galapagos Islands, 1,100 km (680 miles) west of mainland Ecuador. They nest in crevices and caves among rocks, or in burrows dug in the dry sandy soil. Most nest within a few metres of the sea, avoiding the scorching equatorial sun. These, too, are quiet, secretive birds, on land more active by night than by day. Because they appeared so little in the open, biologists thought they were extremely rare and perhaps dying out altogether. Recent surveys have revealed more than expected, but indicate that the population fluctuates widely according to long-term changes in fish stocks close at hand.

Peruvian penguin resting, with flippers almost touching the ground

Peruvian pengu...

Where they live

RELATIONSHIPS

These are the two tropical species of burrowing penguins, closely related to jackass (pages 34-35) and Magellanic penguins (pages 36-37). Peruvian penguins are similar in size and appearance to Magellanics, with a single black bar across the shirt-front and more pink on the face. The species name *humboldti* commemorates the German explorer Friedrich Alexander Humboldt, who spent five years in South America during the early 1800s. Galapagos penguins are smaller, with more hazy, indefinite colour patterns, and two black chest bars similar to Magellanics. Their species name *mendiculus* means 'small beggar', reflecting their size and perhaps their creeping, uncertain way of walking.

Magellanic

Peruvian

Jackass

Galapagos

FEEDING

Peruvian and Galapagos penguins feed on small fish, which they catch in surface waters close to their colonies. They feed on squid and on crustaceans too, but fish form their main diet. The cold currents in which they feed are rich in nutrients. Fish are plentiful, except during periods of El Niño (right), when they become very scarce. Then the penguins and other sea-birds go hungry.

Peruvian penguins breed along the west coast of South America, from Lobos de Tierra in Peru to Valparaiso in central Chile, occasionally nesting even farther south on coasts occupied by Magellanic penguins. Their widely dispersed colonies make counting difficult, but there are estimated to be at least 10,000 breeding pairs, possibly more.

Galapagos penguins breed on Fernandina and Isabela, two of the main Galapagos islands. Small groups and individuals are seen on other islands from time to time, and may even be breeding in out-of-the-way corners. Local biologists, keen to protect the species from interference by visitors, do not tell all they know. There are probably about 5,000-10,000 breeding pairs, still few enough to make this a rare species, needing all the protection we can give.

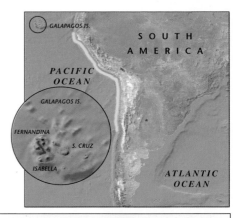

Peruvian penguins	Galapagos penguins

Galapagos penguins in early morning sunshine

GUANO

The desert islands off the Peruvian coast support huge colonies of sea-birds, mainly cormorants, pelicans and penguins. For centuries the droppings of these birds accumulated on the islands, drying in the hot sun to a chalky or crystalline powder. On some islands the powder, called guano, lay 20 m (66 ft) or more thick. During the early 1800s, guano was found to be an excellent agricultural fertilizer.

Thousands of workers were employed on the islands to bag it and export it to the United States and Europe.

Cormorants and pelicans, nesting on the surface of the guano, quickly recovered from the disturbance. Peruvian penguins nested in the guano. When it was taken, thousands were left homeless. By the late 1800s, all the guano deposits had gone, and so had most of the Peruvian penguins.

EL NIÑO

This is a current of warm surface waters that flows south along the northern coast of Ecuador. Every year around Christmas it becomes stronger and extends along the northern coast of Peru, pushing aside the rich, colder waters of the Humboldt Current. El Niño means 'infant' and is named in honour of the infant Jesus. When it appears off Peru, usually for about a month, fish disappear from surface waters, and sea-birds and fishermen have to travel farther for their catches.

Every six or seven years, the patterns of atmospheric pressure that produce the current shift, in ways that make *El Niño* flow stronger,

extend farther south and last several weeks longer. Sea-birds nesting at this time are likely to lose their chicks, and may themselves starve. Every forty or fifty years the patterns change further, causing *El Niño* to flow stronger still, affecting currents aand weather patterns all round the globe. These are years when whole populations of sea-birds, including Peruvian and Galapagos penguins, go hungry. No chicks are reared, and thousands of starved adults are washed up dead on the beaches.

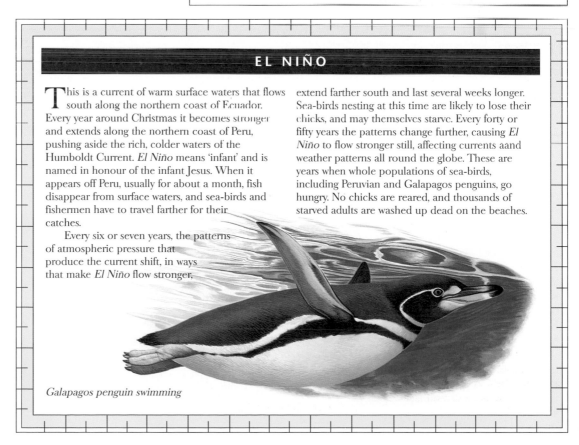

Galapagos penguin swimming

FACT FILE

LITTLE BLUE PENGUIN

Family:	Spheniscidae
Latin name:	*Eudyptula minor*
Colour:	Blue-grey back, white chin, throat and shirt-front, blue-grey flippers
Standing height:	35 cm (14 in)
Flipper length:	10 cm (4 in)
Weight:	Avge 1 kg (2 lb 3 oz); up to 2 kg (4 lb 7 oz)
Breeding range:	Southern Australia, New Zealand, Chatham Islands

WHITE-FLIPPERED PENGUIN

Family:	Spheniscidae
Latin name:	*Eudyptula albosignata*
Colour:	Blue-grey back, white chin, throat and shirt-front, blue-grey flippers edged with white
Standing height:	35 cm (14 in)
Flipper length:	10 cm (4 in)
Weight:	Avge 1.4 kg (3 lb); up to 2 kg (4 lb 7 oz)
Breeding range:	Banks Peninsula, Motunau Island and neighbouring coast of South Island, New Zealand

RELATIONSHIPS

Little blue and white-flippered penguins are the smallest of the family. Little blues breed only in Australia and New Zealand.. Australians call them 'fairy penguins' – just right to express their size and delicate colouring.

Little blues vary slightly from one part of their range to another. Southern blue penguins are darker and more steely-blue than northern. Those on the Chatham Islands are smallest, with stronger bills and shorter feathers.

White-flippered penguins breed locally on and near Banks Peninsula, New Zealand, They are larger, with silvery-blue plumage and conspicuous white edges to their flippers.

THE SMALLEST PENGUINS

Little blue and white-flippered penguins of Australia and New Zealand.

PEOPLE WHO LIVE near the shore in parts of New Zealand or southern Australia, often find little blue penguins wandering in their gardens. In coastal woodlands and consolidated sand dunes, away from civilization, they form big colonies of several hundred scattered nests. Where there are settlements, farms and people, they live in smaller groups, nesting wherever they can find safety from cats, dogs, foxes and other predators.

Little blues look delicate, but this is misleading. If handled, they are well able to look after themselves with sharp bills and flailing flippers. Handling, however, is allowed only with a permit. They are protected by law wherever they live.

Little blue penguins are engaging to have around, but not always good neighbours. They like to dig rabbit-size burrows in soft earth, perhaps in the flower beds. Even more, they like a comfortable dry nest site under a building, especially under a timber-framed house. A New Zealand beach cottage, or 'bach', is ideal. During courtship, from late winter onwards, they may keep residents awake with noisy calls and fighting under the floorboards. In summer they bring home fish for the chicks, some of which may spill and rot. If they or the chicks should die under there, bach owners quickly know about it because of the smell, and may have to take the floor up.

Little blues are not rare birds, but they may well be losing out against the spread of people. Each new shore-side road or housing development, each new wall and garden fence, presents a new problem for the little blue penguins. More dangerous still may be the fishermen who compete for their food.

The rare white-flippered penguin is very similar in habits to the little blue, and some biologists classify it as a subspecies. But in this book we treat it as a separate species.

Little blue penguin on cave nest

Little blue penguin nesting under an old beach shack

Where they live

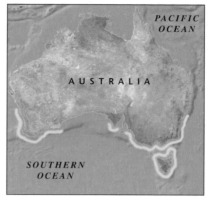

Australian subspecies

Chatham Island

New Zealand subspecies

White-flippered

FEEDING

Little blue penguins leave for the sea around sunrise and forage all day, mainly in surface waters a few kilometres from home. They catch small fish and squid 5-13 cm (2-5 in) long, crab larvae and shrimps, and occasionally squid. Fishing brings them into competition with commercial fishermen, whose nets sweep the same seas. Little blues return to land each evening, usually after sunset, carrying about 85 g (3 oz) of food in their tiny crops.

White-flippered penguin nesting in cave

BREEDING

Little blues live close to their breeding grounds all the year round. Pairs start courtship any time between May and October, and lay between June and late September, with a peak in August and September. Each pair lays two smooth white eggs, in a burrow or under vegetation. The partners share the 36 days of incubation. The two chicks, brown-backed and white-fronted, take about 9 weeks to reach full weight, moult into juvenile plumage and leave for the sea.

White-flippered penguins have similar breeding habits, but breed at slightly different times.

Little blue penguins breed at several points along the south coast of Australia, around Tasmania, and on the coast of New Zealand. Because they stay close to home all the year round and do not wander far, they form several separate populations, which hardly mix at all with each other. As there is little cross-breeding, each group has developed the slight differences that make biologists think of them as subspecies:

Australia
■ Southern coasts, including Tasmania: *Eudyptula minor novaehollandiae*

New Zealand
■ Northern coasts of North Island: *Eudyptula minor iredalei*
■ Southern coasts of North Island, northern coasts of South Island: *Eudyptula minor variabilis*
■ Southern coasts of South Island: *Eudyptula minor minor*
■ Chatham Islands: *Eudyptula minor chathamensis*

Many nest underground, making them difficult to count, but estimates suggest that New Zealand and Australia each have around 30,000 to 40,000 pairs of little blue penguins.

White-flippered penguins, which some regard as a sixth subspecies of little blue, breed very locally on Banks Peninsula, Motunau Island and neighbouring coasts along the eastern shore of New Zealand's South Island. There are probably only a few hundred pairs.

Little blue chick

PENGUINS ON PARADE

Little blue penguins seldom appear during the day. The best chance to see them is to find a place where they live. Local people always know, and footprints across the beach are a giveaway. Walk there in late evenings when they are coming ashore, and early mornings when they are leaving for the sea. Where there are many, they keep together in groups of a dozen or more. If you stand or sit very still, they may come very close. If you flash torches around them or frighten them with

noise, they will scuttle off into the darkness.

At Phillip Island, a breeding area close to Melbourne, Australia, the evening parade ashore has become a major tourist attraction. Lit by floodlights, which seem not to trouble them, hundreds of little blue penguins come ashore each evening, crossing the beach to the delight of several hundred spectators. Hundreds of thousands of people watch the 'show' every year.

The evening parade of little blues

WHAT IS SPECIAL ABOUT PENGUINS?

As thousands of visitors discover each year, penguins are fun to watch. Strutting busily in their grey-black jackets and white shirt-fronts, stumbling on short legs, solemnly picking up feathers and stones, quarrelling and fighting with each other over nests or mates, penguins seem like fussy, pompous little people.

Checking rockhopper penguins in a breeding colony

However, to biologists they are far more interesting than that. They are a very special kind of bird, adapted for life in the sea, with a history far longer than our own (see page 13). Penguins appeared on earth long before the first humans, and have survived huge changes in the shapes of oceans and continents, and major shifts of world climate. Equally at home in some of the world's warmest and coldest seas, they have much to tell us about navigation, living in water, diving, keeping warm in cold climates, and surviving environmental change. By studying how penguins live and behave, we can learn useful things about ourselves.

But just watching them, in the wild or in zoos, can be entertaining and interesting too. You do not need to be a scientist to learn something worth knowing from penguins.

SAVING THE PENGUINS

How scientists work to protect penguins.

THE NATIVE PEOPLE who first met penguins in Africa, South America, Australia and New Zealand were interested mainly in eating them and their eggs. European sailors who discovered them in the 1600s killed many for food. The sealers who followed in the 1700s and 1800s, seeking sealskins and oil on remote southern islands, hunted penguins for their feathers, skin and fat.

King penguins especially were killed and boiled up, making a clear oil that could be sold for burning in lamps. Skins of several species were turned into feathery mats and slippers. Until quite recently, Magellanic penguin skins were tanned to make soft shoe leather.

From the 1800s onwards, scientists killed many hundreds of penguins to study their skeletons and anatomy, to find out what they fed on and how their bodies worked. Collectors captured them for showing in zoos. For every penguin

Jackass penguin

that reached a zoo alive, several others died of injuries or diseases on the way.

Today we do not need to kill penguins for food, oil or any other of the old reasons. Scientists still study them, but are generally more interested in live penguins than dead ones. We try to find ways of studying them without having to handle or frighten them, or keep them captive for more than a few minutes at a time.

Galapagos penguin

Counting, marking and weighing

PENGUINS IN ZOOS

People who live in the northern hemisphere see penguins only in zoos and aquariums. Some people think it is cruel to keep them in captivity.

Taking penguins from the wild, putting them in boxes and shipping them around the world stresses them badly. Many sicken and die before they ever reach the zoo. Not all zoos can afford to look after penguins properly. Of those that survive the journey, many die from poor feeding, or from lung infections caused by breathing dusty air.

However, most penguins that you see in zoos today have been born and bred there. So long as they are well tended and cared for, they may live for many years in captivity. Well fed and free from predators, they may live longer than most penguins in the wild.

They need good food, nesting materials and room for nesting, a large clean pool, and an area of sand or grass for walking on.

COUNTING PENGUINS

It is useful to know how many penguins there are of each species, so that we can judge whether or not they need protection. Scientists usually try to estimate numbers of breeding pairs, as that is a good indication of their success.

Species that nest in the open, such as Adélie and gentoo penguins, are relatively easy to count, directly or by photographing them from aircraft. Those that nest among trees or underground can usually only be estimated.

DIVING AND SWIMMING

Penguins can be fitted with small packages of electronic equipment that tell us how far they travel at sea and how often and how deep they dive, and collect information about their breathing and heart-rate while they are in the water. They can be fitted, too, with radio transmitters that send the information to satellites, and then back to a laboratory anywhere in the world. So a scientist in Europe or the United States can keep track of a penguin swimming and feeding in Antarctic waters.

We can learn much from studying individual penguins. Because they are so alike, we need to mark them individually to tell them apart. One way is to fit metal or plastic bands on their

Scientist examining a penguin

flippers, each with a number or colour code that can be read through binoculars. The bands must be fitted carefully, so they do not damage the birds or interfere with their swimming. Another way is to fit electronic tags or bar codes, which can be checked from a distance by instruments.

From banding and tagging we can find out how long individuals live, which partners they nest with, how often they come ashore, visit the nest or feed their chicks, and where they go when they are at sea.

AUTOMATIC WEIGHING

Where penguins enter and leave a breeding colony by the same path, we can set apparatus in the path that automatically reads each bird's electronic tag, and weighs it as it comes up from the sea and returns. That way we can find out how much each penguin feeds to its chicks, and how its body weight varies through the season. This can be a useful check on the amount of food available in the sea, and

the general welfare of the penguins and their chicks from season to season.

Paint-marked penguin incubating an artificial egg that records its heartbeat (see above)

Conservationists are keen to prevent penguins being disturbed when groups of tourists visit them in the wild. Scientists need to know how much they are affected, especially as more people visit their breeding colonies each year. One way of finding out is to measure the penguins' heart-beat, which slows when they relax but speeds up when they are stressed or anxious. In a breeding colony this is done by fitting an electronic sensor into an artificial egg and placing this in a nest. As the penguin incubates, the sensor records changes in its heartbeat. This allows us to see how much the bird is affected by normal, everyday events – a predator flying over, or another penguin stealing eggs from its nest. Then we can see what happens to the heartbeat when people walk among them, stand and watch, make noises or take photographs.

Generally, if human visitors keep a distance of 4–5 m (13–16 ft) away, and move slowly and quietly around the colony, nesting penguins are very little disturbed by them.

Tourists visiting a penguin colony

Yellow-eyed penguin

GLOSSARY

Can you identify the species pictured?
(answers below)

adapt	Change in ways that make a species more efficient in its environment or surroundings
aggressive	Likely to attack
albumen	The 'white' of the egg, which provides the growing embryo with nutrients
blubber	Layer of fat under the skin of sea-birds and sea mammals
cloaca	Hole in the body wall through which pass faeces (food waste), urine (waste from kidneys) and eggs
colony	Breeding group of penguins or other birds
conservation	Saving and protecting species, usually by protecting the places where they live
crop	First part of a bird's stomach
crustaceans	Invertebrate animals (without backbones) that are covered with tough, jointed shells. They include many kinds of crabs and shrimps.
density	Number (of animals) in a particular area
digestive system	Parts of an animal in which food is broken down and absorbed (mouth, throat, stomach, intestines, etc.)
DNA	The basic substance of life, found in animals and plants, that determines their structure and behaviour and everything else about them. It may also be used to identify a species or individual, or distinguish between male and female
dominant	Most important, able to control others
forage	Search for food
fossil	Remnant of plant or animal preserved in stone
habitat	Place where a plant or animal lives
herbivore	Animal that feeds mainly on vegetation and plant life
incubating	Holding an egg to keep it warm
larvae	Young forms of fish, insects, etc.
mandible	Lower half of the bill
monitoring	Watching carefully to see what progress is being made

From top: Adélie penguin, Peruvian penguin, king penguins

nutrients	Chemical components or parts of food that are essential to health
oviduct	The tube carrying the eggs, or ova, from the ovary to the outside
population	Members of a species living in a particular area, sometimes but not always separated geographically from other populations of the same species (see 'stock')
predator	Fierce animal that hunts, kills and eats other animals
preening	Using the bill to arrange and align the feathers
scavenge	Eat rubbish or old food that has been lying around for some time
soar	Rise in the air without flapping the wings
spawning	Egg-laying
species	A particular kind of plant or animal
stock	Small group of animals or plants of one species, forming part of a population (see 'population')
tussock	Large tuft or clump of grass
zooplankton	Small animals that float in surface waters

Useful addresses WWF (UK), Panda House, Weyside Park, Cattershall Lane, Godalming, Surrey GU7 1XR
Tel: (0)1488 426 444; Fax: (0)1483 426 409

WWF (USA), 1250 24th st NW, Suite 500, Washington DC 20037

WWF (Australia), Level 5, 725 George Street, Sydney, NSW 2000

WWF (South Africa), 116 Dorp Street, Stellenbosch 7600

From top: Emperor penguin chick, rockhopper penguin, yellow-eyed penguin

INDEX